Immigration

DALE HANSON BOURKE

TOUGH QUESTIONS, DIRECT ANSWERS

IVP Books

An imprint of InterVarsity Press
Downers Grove, Illinois

InterVarsity Press
P.O. Box 1400, Downers Grove, IL 60515-1426
World Wide Web: www.ivpress.com
Email: email@ivpress.com

InterVarsity Press® is the book-publishing division of InterVarsity Christian Fellowship/USA®, a movement of students and faculty active on campus at hundreds of universities, colleges and schools of nursing in the United States of America, and a member movement of the International Fellowship of Evangelical Students. For information about local and regional activities, write Public Relations Dept., InterVarsity Christian Fellowship/USA, 6400 Schroeder Rd., P.O. Box 7895, Madison, WI 53707-7895, or visit the IVCF website at www.intervarsity.org.

Scripture quotations, unless otherwise noted, are from the New Revised Standard Version of the Bible, copyright 1989 by the Division of Christian Education of the National Council of the Churches of Christ in the USA. Used by permission. All rights reserved.

While all stories in this book are true, some names and identifying information in this book have been changed to protect the privacy of the individuals involved.

Cover design: Cindy Kiple
Interior design: Beth Hagenberg

ISBN 978-0-8308-4409-8 (print)
ISBN 978-0-8308-7965-6 (digital)

Printed in the United States of America ∞

 As a member of the Green Press Initiative, InterVarsity Press is committed to protecting the environment and to the responsible use of natural resources. To learn more, visit greenpressinitiative.org.

Library of Congress Cataloging-in-Publication Data
A catalog record for this book is available from the Library of Congress.

P	18	17	16	15	14	13	12	11	10	9	8	7	6	5	4	3	2	1
Y	29	28	27	26	25	24	23	22	21	20	19	18	17	16	15	14

Contents

Introduction

My grandparents simply called it "the old country." They rarely talked about the place where they were born or seemed to miss anything about it. The old country was where they were from, but America was where they belonged.

As part of the great wave of immigrants in the early twentieth century, my grandparents arrived on a ship, were processed at Ellis Island in New York and settled into one of the ethnic neighborhoods in Chicago. Like most large American cities, Chicago absorbed a large share of immigrants from Ireland, Italy and Eastern Europe, many fleeing some form of poverty or persecution. They spoke their native language at their neighborhood stores, restaurants, bars and church.

Many of the immigrants, like my grandparents, were poorly educated. They never learned to speak much English and lacked the skills to integrate into society. They worked hard, long hours in factories, service industries or physical labor. Their children, born and raised in the United States, would speak the language of their parents only at home; with their friends they spoke English. Their goal was to leave their ethnic roots behind and merge into the mainstream of America, identifying less as Irish, Italian or Polish and more as Americans.

Much has changed in the century since my grandparents and others of their generation entered the "land of opportunity." Today immigrants to the United States are more likely to come from Latin America or Asia. Few enter via ship or ever see the Statue of Liberty. Many arrive with advanced degrees.

The country that welcomed my grandparents as part of the "tired, poor, huddled masses yearning to breathe free"[1] is now more selective. Entering America is less about finding a place on a ship than about finding a spot in one of the bewildering categories of the legal immigration system—and then hoping the quota doesn't fill before your number comes up.

The front door to America is accessed only through the most complex labyrinth, with many dead ends and blind alleys along the way. The back door, however, has remained temptingly unlocked for many years, offering students and others with temporary visas little incentive to declare themselves "out of status" and return to their countries of origin. And there are windows open as well, for those who cross the border at the right spot or risk their lives on a boat or with a smuggler.

The vast majority of immigrants today are seeking the same things as my grandparents: safety, security and a chance for a better life. But the rules have changed and keep changing. The goal of becoming an American is a moving target. I can only think that my grandparents wouldn't have a chance today—they could never have navigated the complexity of the system in order to live their simple dream.

There has been much talk in the United States about immigration reform. Almost everyone agrees that the immigration system is broken. But how do we fix it? This book is not meant to convince anyone of what should be done. It offers the facts about immigration to date, shows how the issues in the United States are part of global migration issues, and offers some information about how the system works now and what proposals are on the table to improve it.

The book also talks about the more recent immigrants among us. Citizens, green card holders, temporary visitors and the precariously "undocumented"—how do we, citizens of a nation of immigrants, relate to newcomers? How does the church care for those who cannot navigate the complex system and stand with those whose lives are torn apart by rules that often seem contradictory? What is right and just, kind and fair? My hope and prayer is that this book serves as a way to understand immigration and as a guide to move forward.

Acronyms

CBP	Customs and Border Patrol
CPR	Conditional Permanent Resident
DACA	Deferred Action for Childhood Arrivals
DHS	Department of Homeland Security
DOE	Date of Entry
DREAM Act	Development, Relief and Education of Alien Minors Act
GEP	Global Entry Program
ICE	Immigration and Customs Enforcement
IDP	Internally Displaced Persons
INA	Immigration and Nationality Act
INS	Immigration and Naturalization Service (now the USCIS)
ITIN	Individual Taxpayer Identification Number
LEP	Limited English Proficient
LPR	Lawful Permanent Resident
NIV	Non-immigrant Visa
PRC	Permanent Resident Card (Green Card)
RPI	Registered Provisional Immigrant
UNHCR	United Nations High Commissioner for Refugees
USCIS	United States Citizenship and Immigration Service (formerly INS)
USCS	United States Customs Service
VOLAG	Volunteer Agency
VWP	Visa Waiver Program

Refugees from the Democratic Republic of Congo (DRC) try to escape violence.

1. Defining Terms

Even though immigration is a hot topic, there is a great deal of confusion about some of the basic terms associated with it. Here are some of the most important terms used in the immigration debate.

Who is an immigrant?

An immigrant is a person who has left the land of his or her birth and moved to another country with the intention of settling there. Such a person may also be called "foreign born," a term that some people consider to have less stigma than *immigrant*.

An immigrant can be a naturalized citizen, a lawful permanent resident (LPR), a refugee or asylum seeker, or someone who is unauthorized. Generally, those entering the country or remaining in the country are either immigrating legally or illegally.

What is the difference between emigration and immigration?

A person *emigrates* from a country of origin and *immigrates* to another country. The words describe the same act but from different perspectives. *Migration* is the word that describes the movement of people and encompasses *emigration* and *immigration.*

Syrian children now going to school in Lebanon.

Emigration generally refers to a voluntary leaving, although people tend to leave countries because of hardship of some kind and move to countries where there is a chance of living a life of fewer difficulties. Involuntary emigration is involved in situations such as ethnic cleansing or population transfer.

Why do people migrate?

People move from one country or one region to another for many reasons. Some are seeking employment or a better standard of living for their family. Many are fleeing natural disaster (such as the potato famine in the 1800s that brought many Irish families to America) while others are escaping wars or a repressive government.

Many people migrate in order to join other family members or so their children can be born in a country where they will have a better future. Some come to have the opportunity for a better or more advanced education than is available in their home country. Some people visit and then decide to stay.

Why are immigrants sometimes called "aliens"?

Alien is a legal term for a person living in a country in which he or she is not a citizen. A *legal alien* is a person from another country who holds a visa or other documentation making it legal to be in the country. A *resident alien* has documents proving that the person is allowed to reside legally in the country. A *nonresident alien* is a person who is legally visiting (but not residing in) the country.

An *undocumented alien* is a person who does not have legal standing to stay in the country either as a visitor or resident; these immigrants are considered

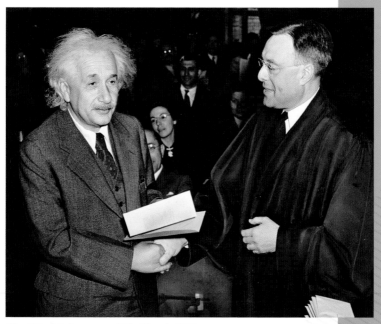

Albert Einstein becomes a U.S. citizen in 1940.

deportable. An *enemy alien* is a citizen of a country considered to be an enemy of the country in which he or she is visiting or residing.

What's wrong with calling someone an "illegal immigrant"?

> *"No State shall . . . deny to any person within its jurisdiction the equal protection of the laws."*
>
> Fourteenth Amendment to the U.S. Constitution

Although it is a commonly used description for a foreign born person who is undocumented, many people consider the terms *illegal immigrant* and *illegal alien* to be dehumanizing. Any person in the United States is a legal person and is protected under the law. Citizens who break the law, for example, remain *legal* persons despite having committed *illegal* acts. Similarly, a person who has violated immigration requirements—who entered the country without proper paperwork, or used forged or stolen documents, or overstayed a visa—is still a legal person under the law.

Under the Fourteenth Amendment of the U.S. Constitution, neither the federal government nor state governments may "deny to any person within its jurisdiction the equal protection of the laws." This part of the Constitution is called the "equal protection" clause because it protects all human beings from being treated as less than a legal person.

The term *illegal immigrant* is no longer used in most media. Calling a person an "undocumented immigrant" is a more accurate way to describe someone who resides in a country without proper documentation.

What does it mean to be undocumented?

In the United States, a person may be called upon in certain cases to prove citizenship, lawful permanent resident status or legal visitor status. In order to prove U.S. citizenship, the person must have a birth certificate, a certificate of citizenship (for a person born abroad to U.S. citizens), a U.S. passport or a naturalization certificate.

The term *undocumented* usually refers to a person's immigration status and means that he or she does not possess documents to prove legal residence or citizenship.

Many countries issue a national identity card or current visa as documentation. The United States doesn't have a national identity card. Other documents that prove a person is in the United States legally include a foreign passport with a valid, unexpired U.S. visa, a permanent resident card (sometimes called a "green card") or an employment authorization card. Generally, neither driver's licenses nor Social Security cards can be used as proof of legal residency.

FACT: *Between 1840 and 1920, approximately 37 million immigrants entered the United States.*

What does it mean to be "out of status"?

A person who is "out of status" in the immigration system is usually in possession of an expired document and therefore no longer considered to be documented; he or she is residing illegally in the country. One of the most common examples is when a person enters the United States on a student visa and then either leaves school or graduates. The terms of the visa require that person—no longer a student—to leave the country or apply for a different type of visa. People in this category are also called "overstays."

Who are refugees?

Refugees are people outside their home country because they are fleeing war or natural disaster, or because they fear persecution based on their race, religion, nationality or political opinion. The United Nations High Commission on Refugees (UNHCR) estimated that there were 11.1 million refugees in the world at the beginning of 2013.[1] While the United Nations designates refugee status under international law, individual countries decide how to recognize refugees and whether they are eligible to be resettled within the country.

Refugees arrive in Seattle to be resettled by World Relief.

Although most cases are considered on an individual basis, sometimes in the case of a mass exodus because of war or persecution, the UNHCR will grant a people group refugee status. Individual countries may then make exceptions to their immigration policies in order to help accommodate the specific group of people.

What is a refugee resettlement agency?

Many countries have specific agencies that help refugees resettle and integrate, assisting them with language skills, jobs and other needs.

The U.S. State Department's Bureau of Population, Refugee and Migration's Reception and Placement Program (R&P) places refugees arriving in the United States with an approved private voluntary agency that oversees the transition of the refugee, especially during the first ninety days.

National agencies in the United States include Church World Service (CWS), Episcopal Migration Ministries (EMM), Ethiopian Community Development Council

Refugee Resettlement Chart. U.S. Government Accountability Office

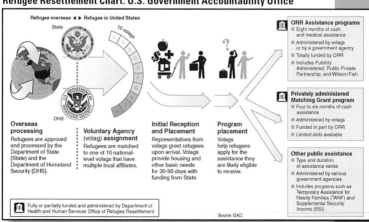

(ECDC), Hebrew Immigration Aid Society (HIAS), International Rescue Committee (IRC), Lutheran Immigration and Refugee Service (LIRS), U.S. Conference of Catholic Bishops (USCCB), U.S. Committee for Refugees and Immigrants (USCRI) and World Relief Corporation (WR). The approved agencies receive funding through both the Department of State and Health and Human Services for each refugee they resettle.

Who are asylum seekers?

According to the United Nations, an asylum seeker is someone whose claim to be a refugee has not yet been definitively evaluated. National asylum systems decide which asylum seekers actually qualify for protection. Countries may have different standards, quotas or other laws regarding asylum seekers and refugees. The United States accepts approximately 40,000 asylum seekers annually.

To qualify for asylum in the United States, an applicant must establish (1) that he or she fears persecution, (2) that persecution would occur because of one of five protected grounds (race, religion, nationality, political opinion or social group) and (3) that the asylum seeker's government is either involved in the persecution or unable to control it.

A woman resettled by World Relief studies English.

How do people prove the need for political asylum?

Proving an individual case of political asylum is often more difficult than showing a pervasive tendency of a government to persecute a racial, religious or ethnic group of people. Political asylum seekers must bring proof that threats have been made against them for specific views or political affiliations, and that there is little or no chance that the situation will change.

Seeking political asylum in the United States almost always requires representation by an attorney well versed in the laws. Once a person enters the asylum process he or she may be detained while the case works its way through the system. The majority of political asylum cases are denied, but appeals are sometimes granted. During the appeal process, the asylum seeker remains in detention.

FACT:
The United States accepts approximately 40,000 asylum seekers each year.

Is it true that people fleeing some countries get special treatment?

U.S. immigration policy has at times recognized certain groups of people who are fleeing particular situations. Preferential treatment is given to Cubans, for example; under the Cuban Adjustment Act of 1966, they are automatically granted legal residency if they reach U.S. soil regardless of how they arrive or whether they can prove persecution. This has led thousands to attempt dangerous journeys by boat to reach the shores of the United States.

At other times in history the United States has either been more lenient with certain groups of people fleeing persecution or raised the quotas for people coming out of countries with documented large-scale persecution. For example, after the Vietnam War, the United States admitted a large number of Vietnamese fleeing their country. More recently, a special exception was granted to Iraqis who had helped the U.S. military and wanted to move to the United States.

What is temporary protected status?

"Everywhere immigrants have enriched and strengthened the fabric of American life."

John F. Kennedy

Temporary protected status (TPS) is granted to people in the United States who cannot return to their home country because of "natural disaster," "extraordinary temporary conditions" or "ongoing armed conflict." Although it is generally granted for six to eighteen months, the status can be extended if unsafe conditions in the country persist. This status has been applied to people from El Salvador, Haiti (after the 2010 earthquake) and, most recently, Syria.

Although the status is meant to protect people temporarily, it has remained in place for some countries well after the threat of conflict or natural disaster has ended. Those covered by the status are allowed to work legally and even travel outside the United States, but they face uncertainty about their long-term immigration status.

How does a person qualify to immigrate legally to the United States?

A person who legally immigrates to the United States is admitted as a lawful permanent resident (LPR). U.S. immigration admissions standards are a complex set of preferences, categories and numerical limits; these change annually, making it difficult for a person to navigate the system. Current categories include refugees and asylum seekers, those reuniting with family members, those who are qualified for employment-based visas, and those considered "diversity immigrants" who qualify for the visa lottery.

What is a "green card"?

A U.S. Permanent Resident card is an identification card attesting to the legal status of a foreign-born person in the United States. It is called a "green card" because from 1946 until 1964, and since May 2010, it has been green in color.

The green card serves as proof that a person is a lawful permanent resident and has been officially granted immigration benefits, including permission to live and work in the United States. The cardholder must maintain

A sample green card.

permanent resident status by living in the United States and can be removed from the country if certain conditions are not met (for example, if the person is convicted of certain crimes).

Permanent Resident Rights & Responsibilities

Your Rights as a Permanent Resident

As a permanent resident (green card holder), you have the right to:
- live permanently in the United States, provided you do not commit any actions that would make you removable under immigration law
- work in the United States at any legal work of your qualification and choosing (although some jobs will be limited to U.S. citizens for security reasons)
- be protected by all laws of the United States, your state of residence and local jurisdictions

Your Responsibilities as a Permanent Resident

As a permanent resident, you are:
- required to obey all laws of the United States, the states and localities
- required to file your income tax returns and report your income to the U.S. Internal Revenue Service and state taxing authorities
- expected to support the democratic form of government and not to change the government through illegal means
- required, if you are a male age eighteen through twenty-five, to register with the Selective Service

"Rights and Responsibilities of a Green Card Holder." From U.S. Citizenship and Immigration Services, Department of Homeland Security website.

Who are migrant workers?

A migrant worker is a person who travels in search of short-term or seasonal work. The U.N. definition refers to "a person who is engaged or has been engaged in a remunerated activity in a State of which he or she is not a national."[2] Other definitions include workers who travel within a country for seasonal work. In China, millions of migrant workers leave the countryside to work in cities or in factory locations. In Europe, residents from poorer European Union countries often work temporarily in countries attracting seasonal tourists. Many U.S. migrant workers are documented, and some are natural-born citizens.

A migrant worker from Africa working in Israel.

Appeals for the rights of migrant workers may overlap with the concerns for the rights of immigrants, but not all migrant workers are immigrants.

Who are guest workers?

People who contract with companies to perform labor in countries with workforce shortages, and who then return home once their contract has expired, are called "guest workers." In many countries guest workers perform domestic, agricultural or other low-income jobs.

A country with a guest worker program allows foreign workers to live and work in a host country for a limited period of time. A person who enters a country as a guest worker is often restricted from seeking more permanent status and may have limited rights to seek national services. Some countries specifically limit the guest worker's family from entering the country.

Civil rights advocates in some countries have raised concerns about the ability of guest workers to seek protection under the law, since they are contractually bound to their employer.

Who is a naturalized citizen?

A person who does not become a citizen at birth becomes a citizen of a country through a process called *naturalization*. The process of naturalization varies by country; the rights of a naturalized citizen may be the same as birthright citizens, or certain restrictions may be placed on naturalized citizens.

Once a person becomes a naturalized U.S. citizen he or she has the right to vote in U.S. elections, participate in federal programs such as Social Security, obtain a U.S. passport and qualify for certain security clearances. A naturalized citizen of the United States may hold any public office except president or vice president. Both Henry Kissinger and Madeleine Albright held the post of secretary of state, generally considered to be fourth in line in the presidential succession plan. Due to restrictions in the U.S. Constitution, however, neither would have been eligible to serve as president or vice president.

FACT:
A person not born in the United States becomes a citizen through naturalization.

Former Secretary of State Madeleine Albright, a naturalized U.S. citizen.

Is "natural-born citizen" the same as naturalized citizen?

Article Two of the U.S. Constitution uses the phrase "natural born" to describe eligibility for holding the offices of president or vice president. The exact meaning of that term has been debated and has sometimes been interpreted as being born on U.S. soil as opposed to being a "naturalized citizen." There have been questions about the eligibility of someone who was not born on U.S. soil to hold the highest offices, especially if both parents were not U.S. citizens at the time. Recently questions arose over the eligibility of Senators John McCain (who was born in Panama to U.S. citizens) and Ted Cruz (born in Canada with one parent a U.S. citizen) to seek the presidency. (President Obama was born on U.S. soil to an American mother and a British citizen father.) Various legal scholars hold differing opinions and many believe the courts will ultimately decide the exact meaning.

> *"No Person except a natural born Citizen, or a Citizen of the United States, . . . shall be eligible to the Office of President."*
>
> Article Two, U.S. Constitution

What is a temporary or visitor visa?

Many countries in the world require a person who is visiting as a tourist to first obtain a visa before entering the country. Most countries require a visa if a person is staying more than a short period of time, will be entering and leaving the country multiple times, or is planning to study in the country.

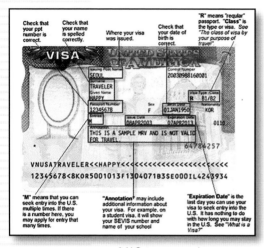

A U.S. temporary visa.

There are currently twenty-four major visitor visa categories and seventy specific types of visas for entering the United States on a temporary basis, a system that is unusually complex.[3] These categories include *tourist, student, temporary worker, person seeking medical treatment, foreign military or diplomatic personnel, journalist, cultural exchange* and *performer.* Each visa has specific requirements and time limits. Some visas are eligible to be extended, but others require a person to return to his or her own country and apply for a new visa.

Most visas are considered "non-immigrant" visas, meaning a person is allowed to enter the country but must leave again and is ineligible to seek more permanent status. These temporary visas are generally known by a letter and number such as B-1 (tourist) and F-1 (foreign student).

Countries Exempted from Visas to Enter United States

Andorra	Finland	Japan	New Zealand	Slovenia
Australia	France	Latvia	Norway	South Korea
Austria	Germany	Liechtenstein	Portugal	Spain
Belgium	Greece	Lithuania	Republic of Malta	Sweden
Brunei	Hungary	Luxembourg	San Marino	Switzerland
Czech Republic	Iceland	Monaco	Singapore	Taiwan
Denmark	Ireland	Netherlands	Slovakia	United Kingdom
Estonia	Italy			

What is the Visa Waiver Program for entering the United States?

The Visa Waiver Program (VWP) allows persons from thirty-seven countries to visit the United States without a visa. Citizens of these countries can stay in the United States for up to ninety days under certain conditions (for example, they must have a current passport containing an electronic chip). Countries include Australia, France, Singapore and the United Kingdom, among others.

What is Ellis Island?

Ellis Island is located in New York Harbor and was the processing center for millions of immigrants who came to the United States (mostly by boat) between 1892 and 1954. Today it houses a museum.

The Statue of Liberty is located on Liberty Island, a short distance from Ellis Island.

Ellis Island arrivals.

Syrian refugees living in a U.N. camp.

2. The Big Picture

The United States isn't the only country in the world dealing with immigration issues. Taking a broader look at world migration helps put things in perspective.

What does it mean to be a citizen?

Citizenship signifies a specific relationship between a person and a state or other political entity. The relationship goes beyond family or tribal ties and generally includes the expectation of participation in a political process, military service and other responsibilities. In return, a citizen receives certain rights, privileges and protections from the state.

Citizenship also implies inclusion and exclusion. A person who is not a citizen is excluded from rights and privileges—and in some cases protection—from the state.

Is nationality the same as citizenship?

Although it is often used interchangeably with *citizenship, nationality* is not legally the same. *Nationality* refers to a legal relationship between a person and a nation that confers certain rights and privileges but may

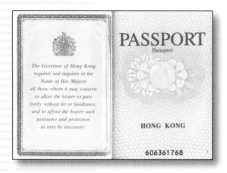

or may not include citizenship. British law includes six categories of nationals, only one being a British citizen, and each having varying rights and privileges. All U.S. citizens are nationals, but not all nationals are U.S. citizens. People born in some U.S. territories or possessions, such as American Samoa, are considered U.S. nationals but are not citizens.

A recent court case in Israel challenged the definition of nationality based on ethnicity instead of citizenship. A Jewish citizen of Israel petitioned the court to have his nationality listed as Israeli not Jewish, as it currently states on his passport. Other citizens of Israel are listed as Arab or "other" instead of Israeli.[1] The court upheld the current definition, but the case has led to an active debate over how nationality is defined.

How do most countries decide if a person is a citizen?

There are, historically, two primary paths to citizenship. The most common (*jus sanguinis,* Latin for "right of blood") is based on family ties; a person born to a family where one or both parents are citizens of a country is granted citizenship in that country, even if he or she was born outside the physical territory of the country. *Jus sanguinis* is common in countries with civil law and may apply for a certain number of generations.

The other path to citizenship (*jus soli*, Latin for "right of soil") is based on physical presence in the country at the time of birth. Some countries that have historically observed *jus soli* have added restrictions (such as that one parent must be a citizen at the time of birth) in order to curb illegal immigration.

In most countries, a person may also become a citizen through marriage or naturalization. The process for these paths varies depending on the country.

FACT:
Most countries in the world grant citizenship based on jus sanguinis ("right of blood"), or parental citizenship.

Do you automatically become a citizen in most countries if you are born there?

A minority of countries grants citizenship based on *jus soli*. There are approximately thirty countries in the world where this is the practice, including the United States and Canada. Most of the rest are in South America.

Of the countries in the world considered "advanced economies" by the International Monetary Fund (IMF), the United States and Canada are the only two countries that offer citizenship based on birth in the country. Great Britain abandoned this policy in 1983, so being born in England, Ireland or Scotland no longer entitles a person to citizenship (unless the parents are citizens or legal residents).

Many countries have restrictions on citizenship

Dark blue: Unconditional birthright citizenship for persons born in the country. Lighter blue: Birthright citizenship with restrictions. Light blue: Birthright citizenship abolished.

for those born in the country who are not children of citizens. Besides being born "on the soil" the person may have to wait until a certain age, prove residence or satisfy other criteria before citizenship is granted.

Why does a person become a citizen of the United States just because he or she is born in the country?

The United States is one of the countries in the world that grants citizenship automatically both to children born to parents who are citizens *and* to children born to non-citizens on U.S. soil. This latter status is known as *birthright citizenship*. (The exception is children born in the United States to diplomats from other countries.)

So the United States grants citizenship based on both *jus soli* and *jus sanguinis.*

Do most countries allow dual citizenship?

It depends on the country and the circumstances. The United States allows citizens to hold dual citizenship in another country as long as that country does not require a person to revoke all other citizenships. About half of the countries in the world offer dual citizenship.

Who are indigenous peoples?

Although there is no universally accepted definition of *indigenous,* the term is often used to describe tribal or native people who are tied to a land and have a distinct culture and language. In most countries they are a minority, but in Bolivia and Guatemala they make up more than half of the population.

According to U.N. estimates, there are approximately 370 million indigenous people in the world, belonging to five thousand different groups in ninety different countries. The majority lives in Asia. Examples would be U.S. Native Americans, the aboriginal people of Australia and the Massai people in East Africa.

Citizenship has in some cases been overtly denied to indigenous peoples. In some countries the indig-

FACT:
There are as many as 370 million indigenous people in the world.

enous people have not participated in formal legal or government programs, including registering births, deaths and other life events, which is how citizenship is conventionally established.

What is the Universal Declaration of Human Rights?

After the massive displacement of people that took place during World War II, the United Nations established the 1948 Universal Declaration of Human Rights. Article Fifteen relates to nationality:

(1) Everyone has the right to a nationality.

(2) No one shall be arbitrarily deprived of his nationality nor denied the right to change his nationality.

After the 2010 earthquake, many Haitians became internally displaced people (IDPs).

Do most countries accept refugees?

Under international law, no country is required to accept refugees. The United States generally receives the highest total number of refugees of all countries, but on a per capita basis Australia and Canada resettle a larger number compared to their population. Norway, Finland, Denmark, Iceland, the Netherlands, Ireland and New Zealand also resettle large numbers of refugees per capita.

The United Nations administrate a number of refugee camps throughout the world. These camps are established in host countries, but refugees are not typically resettled into the host country. In some countries refugees are allowed to leave the camps to work, attend school or seek medical treatment, but some countries do not allow refugees to leave the camps at all. The civil war in Syria led to the creation of the Al-Zaatari refugee camp near Jordan's northern border with Syria, currently the second largest refugee camp in the world. Dadaab in Kenya, which houses those fleeing violence in Somalia, remains the largest.[2]

FACT: There are nearly four thousand stateless people or "citizens of nowhere" in the United States today.

What is refoulement?

Refoulement means the expulsion of a legal refugee from a host country. According to the U.N. Convention, "No Contracting State shall expel or return (*refouler*) a refugee in any manner whatsoever to the frontiers of territories where his life or freedom would be threatened on account of his race, religion, nationality, membership of a particular social group or political opinion."[3]

The principle of non-refoulement forbids the expulsion of refugees to their country of origin or to any country in which they might be subject to persecution. The only exception is if the person to be expelled constitutes a danger to national security in the host country.

What does it mean to be "stateless"?

An individual who is not considered as a national by any state is considered "stateless." People are stateless for a variety of reasons, including discrimination by some countries against minority groups, failure to include all residents as citizens when a state becomes independent, conflicts of laws between states, and failure of individuals to file documents that confirm their citizenship.

An estimated 12 million people worldwide are stateless, according to the UNHCR. A person who is stateless may lack access to health and education services, employment, and the ability to enter into some legal transactions. In many cases, stateless people are exploited because they do not fall under the protection of the laws providing rights to nationals.

Who are internally displaced persons?

Like refugees, internally displaced persons (or IDPs) have fled their home because of natural disaster, war, persecution or other difficult conditions. Unlike refugees, however, IDPs remain within the borders of their own country. According to the United Nations, at the end of 2011 there were an estimated 26.4 million internally displaced people around the world.

What does globalization have to do with immigration?

Globalization essentially erases borders and boundaries between countries, allowing the free flow of information, capital and sometimes goods. It allows connectivity between peoples and markets and is made increasingly possible by the Internet.

Some economists believe the next natural step in

Cambodia border crossing.

globalization is to open labor markets and let people "flow" to wherever jobs occur. This would mean opening borders to economic immigration, a concept that has been part of the experiment in the European Union, where workers are free to move among countries and seek work without formally applying for visas or seeking special documents in order to apply for jobs.

What is free trade and free migration?

Free trade allows goods to flow freely between countries without tariffs, subsidies, quotas or other restrictions. Free migration is the theory that people should be able to move back and forth between countries without cost (such as payment for visas) or quotas.

A free trade zone in Shanghai, China.

What is UNHCR?

The Office of the United Nations High Commissioner for Refugees (UNHCR), also known as the U.N. Refugee Agency, has as its mandate to protect and support refugees at the request of a government or the United Nations itself, and to assist in voluntary repatriation, local integration or resettlement to a third country. Headquartered in Geneva, Switzerland, it is responsible for all refugees and internally displaced persons in the world—with the exception of the Palestinians, whose refugee population of more than 5 million people is administered by the U.N. Relief and Works Agency for Palestine Refugees in the Near East (UNRWA).

The U.N. Refugee Agency supplies emergency goods and shelter to refugees.

Do all countries defend their borders?

Borders are important to countries for various reasons, and countries have the right under international law to restrict and defend their recognized borders. Most countries offer designated border crossing points where persons and goods may enter a country. In general, persons need some type of visa or other paperwork in order to cross a border, and there may be a tax levied

The Coast Guard helps patrol U.S. borders.

on goods crossing a border. Anyone who crosses a border at an undesignated point may be considered hostile or criminal.

Many countries rely on natural barriers for their border security. Australia, for example, does not secure its physical borders (except against unauthorized incoming vessels and airplanes) because it is bordered by ocean on all sides. Other countries, including the United States, have relatively long and easily crossed borders. In many cases, such borders are secured by walls, fences and other physical barriers. Border security has become a major concern in the United States.

There are some famous heavily guarded borders, such as the one between North and South Korea and the infamous one between India and Pakistan at Wagah, where the elaborate daily closing ceremony draws crowds on both sides. In other parts of the world, border crossings range from difficult to routine.

Have any countries relaxed border security?

Some of the countries in the European Union are experimenting with establishing one external border around the countries and relaxing the borders between countries. Travelers in the Schengen area (twenty-six European

FACT: European Union countries have relaxed border restrictions.

Countries in the Schengen Area

Austria	Hungary	Norway
Belgium	Iceland	Poland
Czech Republic	Italy	Portugal
Denmark	Latvia	Slovakia
Estonia	Liechtenstein	Slovenia
Finland	Lithuania	Spain
France	Luxembourg	Sweden
Germany	Malta	Switzerland
Greece	Netherlands	

Schengen border crossing sign.

countries that have removed all internal border controls) can move freely within the area without having to show their passports. Strict border controls are in place for travelers crossing the external borders of the Schengen area, but there are almost no controls within the region. The Schengen-area countries are made up of twenty-two out of the twenty-seven European Union (EU) countries as well as four non-EU countries. The area takes its name from the town of Schengen in Luxembourg, where the original agreement to create a borderless European travel area was signed.

Is there prejudice in most countries against immigrants?

In almost every country and throughout history, the most recent group of immigrants has experienced formal or informal prejudice. Sometimes discrimination occurs because the new immigrants lack communication and cultural skills that would allow them to assimilate. Often immigrants come from neighboring countries viewed as having undesirable traits or where a history of hostility has tainted relations between countries. Sometimes immigrants, unable to find jobs in a new country, are viewed as lazy or indigent. If immigrants have physical features different from the majority population, dress differently or have starkly different customs, they may be singled out and experience prejudice and even abuse.

What is nativism?

Nativism is a movement that promotes favored status for established citizens or residents of a nation over newcomers or immigrants. Nativists typically oppose immigration and support restricting the legal status of specific ethnic groups because they view them as harming the culture of the host nation.

What is xenophobia?

Xenophobia is defined as the fear or hatred of strangers or foreigners. Generally it means a strong dislike for people who are not native born. It often includes prejudices formed on racial, ethnic, religious, cultural or national grounds. Xenophobia often leads to exclusion of certain people because of their perceived attributes associated with a different culture. While xenophobia and racism often overlap, they are different. Racism is generally based on physical differences, such as skin color, but xenophobia implies behavior based on the idea that the person is foreign to the community or nation.

What are national identity cards?

A national identity card is a portable identification card generally including a person's photo, address, and possibly fingerprints or other means of identifying the person. Many countries in the world have national identity cards which every citizen (and most permanent residents) must carry on their person at all times. The card generally identifies the person's citizenship status and other important information.

"It's hard to find countries without ID cards," said Simon Davies, the director of Privacy International, based in England. "It's safe to say that the majority of countries have some kind of national identification system."[4] Civil liberties groups generally oppose national identification cards, while law enforcement officials generally support them. There are no national requirements for a U.S. citizen to carry an identity card of any kind.

Use of national identity cards in the United States has been debated for many years. In early February 2013, the *Washington Post* editorial board ran a column titled "The Case for a National Identity Card." *Forbes* magazine responded with an article titled "We Don't Need a National ID Card," arguing instead for an improved system of identifica-

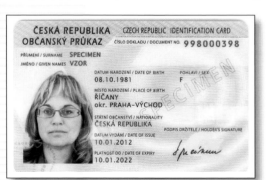

Czech Republic national identity card.

tions—"regardless of what happens with immigration reform. Every single day people are inconvenienced, marginalized, and find themselves victims of identity theft because of our country's faulty identity systems."[5]

According to a 2006 Pew research poll, 57 percent of Americans favor having a mandatory national identity card. This was a lower percentage than favored such a policy soon after the terror attacks in September 2001.

How does a person lose citizenship?

Losing citizenship generally only occurs in countries that prohibit dual citizenship and require a person becoming a citizen of a new country to renounce previous citizenship. It is difficult to lose citizenship in the United States, since the law and recent court rulings prohibit taking a person's citizenship against his or her will. Moving to another country for a long period of time, taking a job with a foreign government or marrying a foreign national do not automatically affect your citizenship.

However, if you take a job in another country that requires you to swear an oath of allegiance to that country above all others, serve in the armed forces of a country at war with the United States, commit an act of treason or formally renounce your citizenship, you may lose your U.S. citizenship and no longer enjoy the protection of the United States.

"Immigration is the sincerest form of flattery."

Jack Parr

How do most countries deal with international adoptions?

Many countries forbid the adoption of children by non-citizens or anyone who would take the child outside the country of his or her birth. Other countries have added restrictions on potential adoptions, including age, education, health and financial requirements of adoptive parents.

The Hague Adoption Convention on the Protection of Children and Co-operation in Respect of Inter-Country Adoption (Hague Adoption Convention) is an international agreement that sets practices to safeguard children during intercountry adoptions. It has been in force in the United States since 2008.

The Hague Adoption Convention applies to all adoptions between the United States and the other countries that have joined it. It requires that countries establish a central authority to ensure that the child is legally eligible for adoption and that adoption is in the best interest of the child. The central authority is also responsible to prevent the abduction, sale or trafficking of children. The U.S. State Department is the central authority that oversees these policies in the United States.

What is human trafficking?

Human trafficking is the illegal trading of persons without their consent for the purposes of sexual slavery, forced labor, organ retrieval and other harmful activities. It is estimated to be a $32 billion annual worldwide business that affects as many as 2.4 million people each year.[6]

Persons without legal status in a country, including the undocumented and those who are stateless, are considered particularly vulnerable to human traffickers. Individuals who seek to emigrate often fall into the hands of traffickers who claim to be facilitating immigration but are, in fact, involved in human trafficking.

Who is a "third country national"?

A third country national (TCN) is a person who is employed by an entity (usually an international corporation or humanitarian organization) but is not a citizen of the home country of the organization or the host country. Specific laws and treaties govern which country's labor laws and taxation apply to third country nationals.

"Our fight against human trafficking is one of the great human rights causes of our time."

U.S. President
Barack Obama

Justice for Immigrants NOW!!!
We Are America
New American Opportunity Campaign
www.cirnow.org

3. A Nation of Immigrants

What is the state of immigration and immigrants in the United States today? What is actually known about immigrants, and how does the U.S. immigration policy compare to other countries?

Does the United States have more immigrants than other countries?

The United States does have a greater inflow of immigrants than any other country in the world, with an average of one million new immigrants each year. However, because the U.S. population is so great, as a percentage of population the country ranks twenty-third among countries receiving immigrants.[1]

How many immigrants are in the United States?

A poll by the Pew Research Center released in September 2013 estimated the total number of immigrants in 2012 at more than 41.7 million people, with 11.7 million considered undocumented.[2]

How do most immigrants enter the United States?

"DHS [the
Department
of Homeland
Security] does
not have
reliable data
on emigration
from the
United States."

Congressional
Research Service,
2010

Most immigrants enter the United States legally, either under one of the approved immigration categories or using a short-term visa to enter the country at an airport or ship terminal as a tourist, student, short-term worker or performer. (At this stage a person is considered a "non-immigrant," since these visas are only available to people who do not intend to stay long term.) If a person stays beyond the term of his or her visa and does not seek a renewal or new status, the person becomes undocumented (or out of status) and is residing illegally in the United States.

Illegal entry into the United States generally occurs by crossing a border from Canada or Mexico or by boat, often from the Caribbean. The other most common methods of illegal entry include the use of fraudulent documents to enter the country and fraudulent asylum claims.

A person may enter the United States legally, through either an immigration visa or a non-immigrant visa, and then move to illegal status by overstaying their visa or violating the conditions of the immigration visa. (Committing a crime, for example, is a violation of an immigration visa.) Or a person may enter the country illegally from the start. In both instances a person is considered to be breaking the law, but there may be a difference in the way the two groups are viewed legally.

How many people are in the United States illegally because they overstayed their visa?

There are no exact figures, but the best estimate is that of the nearly 12 million undocumented residents, nearly half have overstayed their legal visa.

Until recently, a visitor entering the United States would fill out a form I-94. Upon leaving the country, that person was to turn in the form to show evidence of emigration. Unfortunately, the paper forms were not very reliable—people could turn in more than one in some cases. The system was recently replaced with an electronic version, which should help track arrivals and departures for those individuals who have entered the country since early 2013. But the status of those who entered previously is not easily obtained. According to a 2010 report to Congress, "DHS [Department of Homeland Security] does not have reliable data on emigration from the United States."[3]

*FACT:
25.8 million people visited the United States from overseas in 2011.*

How many visitors enter the United States each year?

According to the State Department, 7.5 million visitors obtained visas to visit the United States in 2011. Another 18.3 million entered from one of the countries covered by the Visa Waiver Program (VWP).[4]

How do countries qualify for the Visa Waiver Program?

To qualify for the VWP, a country must meet a range of qualifications, including offering reciprocal privileges to U.S. citizens and issuing their nationals machine-readable passports that incorporate biometric identifiers. Anyone entering under the VWP must present a machine-readable passport.

How many people become U.S. citizens each year?

In 2012, 757,434 individuals became naturalized citizens of the United States.[5] This is about average, after a high of more than 1 million in 2008 and less than 500,000 for most years before 2003.[6]

Recent immigrants study for the citizenship test.

Why do people become citizens?

In 2012 an estimated 8.2 million legal permanent residents were eligible to become citizens but had not. Several organizations are trying to encourage this group to seek citizenship because of the perceived hostile environment against some immigrant populations.

Being a lawful permanent resident (LPR) offers many but not all benefits of being a citizen to U.S. residents. A person who becomes a citizen has the right to remain in the United States permanently without renewing his or her status and no longer risks being deported if convicted of a crime. A citizen has full access to government benefits, often has better tax benefits, is eligible for more federal jobs and may seek public office (except for that of president or vice president). A U.S. citizen has a higher priority than an LPR for bringing relatives to the United States and is currently allowed to sponsor siblings for a green card. And a U.S. citizen is eligible to vote and otherwise participate fully in the democratic process.

> "Immigration is not just compatible with but is a necessary component of economic growth."
>
> Congressman Dave Reichert

Where are most new naturalized U.S. citizens from originally?

The largest number of new U.S. citizens in 2012 came from Mexico, followed by the Philippines, India, the Dominican Republic, the People's Republic of China, Cuba, Colombia, Vietnam and Haiti.[7]

How do I know if someone is a citizen or in the United States legally?

Individuals with or without legal status in the United States do not look different from one another or have any particular characteristics that set them apart. A person is not required to speak English in order to become a lawful permanent resident (LPR), or to obtain a Social Security card or, in some states, a driver's license. In general, you are not allowed to ask a person about their citizenship or legal status when considering them for a job.

On the other hand, a person may have obtained a driver's license, Social Security card, student ID or other documents while in legal status and may have not maintained that status. Or a person may not have any of those documents and still be a legal resident.

Is a person's immigration status affected by serving in the military?

U.S. military service is open to American citizens and certain lawful permanent residents (LPRs) of the United States. No one can join the military without first proving LPR status, so serving in the military does not change one's status. It does, however, provide for an expedited process to become a citizen. The residency requirement is waived for applicants in the military.

Members of the U.S. Army becoming citizens.

All men ages eighteen to twenty-five who are residing in the United States (except those on diplomatic passports) are required by law to register with the Selective Service—even if they are undocumented. Those who have not registered may be disqualified from an eventual "pathway to citizenship."[8]

Does marrying a U.S. citizen mean you become a U.S. citizen?

If a foreign national marries a U.S. citizen and is in the country legally, the person may then apply for a green card (lawful permanent resident status). If the person has not entered the country legally or is out of status, the process is more difficult. Once a person receives a green card, if all other conditions are met, she or he may apply for citizenship three years later based on the family relationship. Under most other circumstances, the wait is five years.

Under current law, same-sex marriage is not included in this provision.

How does the U.S. government keep track of immigrant students?

"I will support and defend the Constitution and the laws of the United States of America against all enemies, foreign and domestic."

The Oath of Citizenship

The Department of Homeland Security (DHS) established the Student Exchange Visitor Program (SEVP) to specifically keep track of anyone in the United States on a student visa. The Student Exchange and Visitor Information System (SEVIS) is a database that allows SEVP to track international students, foreign exchange visitors and others, and to log any change of status (such as taking too few classes to qualify or failing to meet a minimum grade requirement).

Schools where foreign students are enrolled are required to report any changes in a student's name, address, major, degree level, funding or work status, and if a student is suspended, fails or drops out of the program.

Penalties for failing to report a change of status or filing false information are severe, and a school that is found to be in violation could lose its ability to enroll students who come to the United States on a student visa.

What qualifies a person living overseas to legally immigrate to the United States?

There are a number of ways a person may qualify to immigrate legally. The most common is based on a family relationship: the applicant is the spouse, child, son- or daughter-in-law, parent or sibling of a U.S. citizen or (more often) lawful permanent resident. The second most common way is to apply for asylum or refugee status. Employment-based preferences is the third most common basis for legal immigration.

FACT:
Most people qualify to immigrate because of family relationships.

When children are adopted from overseas what do they have to do to become U.S. citizens?

International adoptions are governed by U.S. laws, the laws of the child's country of origin and the Hague Convention. The process may be complicated or relatively straightforward, depending on the child's country of origin. The U.S. Department of State has a website dedicated to helping adoptive parents walk through the process: http://adoption.state.gov/adoption_process.php.

The Child Citizenship Act of 2000 streamlined the naturalization process for any child under age eighteen who is (a) adopted by at least one U.S. citizen parent and (b) is in the custody of the citizen parent(s). That child is now automatically naturalized once admitted to or legally adopted in the United States.

What are the basic requirements for a person to become a U.S. citizen?

According to the U.S. Citizenship and Immigration Services, someone who has been a lawful permanent resident and wishes to become a naturalized citizen must

- be at least eighteen years old
- be a lawful permanent resident for three or five years (depending on status)
- have continuous residence and physical presence in the United States for at least thirty months
- be a person of good moral character (not be convicted of certain types of crimes)

Oath of U.S. Citizenship

I hereby declare, on oath, that I absolutely and entirely renounce and abjure all
    allegiance and fidelity to any foreign prince, potentate, state, or sovereignty,
    of whom or which I have heretofore been a subject or citizen;
that I will support and defend the Constitution and the laws of the United States
    of America against all enemies, foreign and domestic;
that I will bear true faith and allegiance to the same;
that I will bear arms on behalf of the United States when required by the law;
that I will perform non-combatant service in the Armed Forces of the United
    States when required by the law;
that I will perform work of national importance under civilian direction when
    required by the law; and
that I take this obligation freely, without any mental reservation or purpose of
    evasion;
so help me God.

- have a basic knowledge of the U.S. government (as determined by the U.S. citizenship test)
- be able to read, write and speak basic English (there are exceptions to this requirement)
- be willing to recite the Oath of Citizenship

What is the U.S. citizenship test?

The U.S. citizenship test gauges an applicant's command of the English language and comprehension of the form and function of the U.S. government, as well as the responsibilities of citizenship.

Applicants are tested on their speaking ability (to determine their ability to understand and speak English), their reading level (applicants must read aloud one of three sentences correctly), and their writing level (applicants must write one out of three sentences correctly).

U.S. citizenship test.

The civics portion of the citizenship test is conducted orally. A candidate is asked up to ten questions from a list of one hundred multiple choice questions provided ahead of time. The person must answer six out of ten questions correctly to pass the civics portion of the naturalization test. Sample questions include

- How many amendments are there in the U.S. Constitution?

- Who is in charge of the executive branch of government?

- What is the term of a U.S. senator?

A person has two chances per application to take the tests. If a person fails part of the test, retesting for that part of the test is scheduled within sixty to ninety days.

Doesn't the U.S. Constitution define citizenship?

The U.S. Constitution contains several references to citizenship (primarily in the qualifications for president, vice president and members of Congress) but, surprisingly, does not define who a citizen actually is. Since the United States followed British common law, the assumption was that a person born on American soil was a citizen. In 1790 Congress passed laws giving citizenship to children born on foreign soil if their father was a U.S. citizen.

The Fourteenth Amendment (passed in 1868) is the first explanation of American citizenship. Section 1 of the amendment states that "all persons born or naturalized in the United States, and subject to the jurisdiction thereof, are citizens of the United States and of the State wherein they reside." The Fourteenth Amendment was passed to guarantee citizenship to slaves who were freed after the Civil War and states that any child born in the United States becomes a citizen at birth.

If a child is not born on U.S. soil and only one parent is a U.S. citizen, is the child a citizen?

A child born on U.S. soil is a citizen whatever the status of his or her parents, and a child born to parents who are both U.S. citizens is a citizen regardless of the place of birth. But a child born outside the United States with only one citizen parent is in a more complicated situation. That child may or may not be a citizen based on factors that include the marital status of the parents and the length of time that the U.S. citizen parent resided in the United States before the child was born.

Ted Cruz was born in Canada to an American mother and a Cuban father.

Why is there so much interest in where candidates for president were born?

"Permit me to hint, whether it would be wise and seasonable to provide a strong check to the admission of Foreigners into the administration of our national Government; and to declare expressly that the Commander in Chief of the American army shall not be given to nor devolve on, any but a natural born Citizen."

John Jay, in a letter to George Washington

The U.S. Constitution states that the president of the United States must be a "natural-born citizen," the meaning of which has been debated for many years. There has never been a definitive court ruling.

According to a Congressional Research Service report, "The overwhelming evidence of historical intent, general understandings, and common law principles underlying American jurisprudence . . . indicate that the most reasonable interpretation of 'natural-born' citizens would include those who are considered U.S. citizens 'at birth' or 'by birth,' . . . including those born abroad of U.S. citizen-parents. This general historical understanding and interpretation is supported, as well, by specific federal case law in the United States, and in official legal opinions of U.S. officers."[9]

Every president to date was born in the United States, although some presidential candidates were not (George Romney was born in Mexico, John McCain in the Panama Canal Zone). Every president except two (Chester A. Arthur and Barack Obama) had two U.S.-citizen parents. Senator Ted Cruz, who was born in Canada to an American mother and Cuban father (who later became a U.S. citizen), has stated his interest in becoming a presidential candidate. Because of his mother's status at the time of his birth, he is considered qualified to run as a "natural-born citizen."

Are people born in Puerto Rico U.S. citizens?

Anyone born in Puerto Rico, Guam or the U.S. Virgin Islands is a U.S. citizen. However, citizens of these U.S. territories (called "insular areas") are not eligible to vote in presidential elections or to elect a member of the U.S. Congress. Residents of American Samoa and Swains Island, also U.S. territories, are not citizens. Residents of insular areas do not pay U.S. federal income taxes, but they do pay Social Security, Medicare and federal commodity taxes.

FACT:
Anyone born in Puerto Rico is a U.S. citizen.

The flags of the United States of America and Puerto Rico.

History of U.S. Immigration Legislation

1790	Congress passes an act requiring two years residency in the United States before qualifying for citizenship.
1795	The residency period required for citizenship is raised from two years to five.
1798	Congress passes four laws called the Alien and Sedition Acts targeting French sympathizers and providing for deportation.
1800	The Alien Act, one of the four Alien and Sedition Acts, is allowed to expire.
1802	The Naturalization Act, one of the four Alien and Sedition Acts, is repealed.
1862	Congress passes the first law restricting immigration, forbidding American vessels to transport Chinese immigrants to the United States.
1875, 1882, 1892	Immigration laws of 1875, 1882 and 1892 provide for the exclusion of various categories of potential immigrants, including convicts, polygamists, prostitutes, those with contagious diseases, and persons liable to become public charges.
1882	Congress passes the Chinese Exclusion Act suspending entry of most Chinese immigrants and providing for deportation of some already in the United States.
1885-1891	The Alien Contract Labor Laws of 1885, 1887, 1888 and 1891 prohibit immigrants from entering the United States to work under contracts made before their arrival.
1891	Congress creates the Immigration and Naturalization Service (INS).
1892	The INS opens an immigration screening station at Ellis Island.
1907	The Japanese government agrees to not issue passports to laborers intending to enter the United States; the U.S. government agrees not to exclude Japanese immigrants until 1924.
1917	Congress passes the Immigration Act, enlarging the classes of aliens excludable from U.S. immigration, including the illiterate and those who are mentally ill.
1918	Congress passes the Anarchist Act of 1918, which expands the exclusion of "subversive aliens."
1921	Congress establishes an annual immigration quota system based on a percentage of current immigrant populations in the United States.
1924	Congress passes the Immigration Act of 1924, changing the basic immigration quotas and helping "preserve the ideal of American homogeneity."
1941	Congress passes an act that refuses visas to foreigners who might endanger public safety in the judgment of a U.S. diplomat or consular officer.
1943	Congress passes a bill repealing the laws restricting Chinese immigrants from entering the United States. Up to 105 Chinese immigrants are allowed to enter the country annually based on the existing quota system.
1945	The War Brides Act allows limited admission of wives and children of citizens honorably discharged or serving in the U.S. armed forces during World War II.
1946	A federal law authorizes the immigration of Filipinos and East Indians.
1948	The Displaced Persons Act of 1948 permits the immigration to the United States of 202,000 Europeans driven from their homes before and during World War II.

1952	The Immigration and Nationality Act incorporates most of the existing laws relating to immigration and abolishes the ban on Asian immigrants.
1965	Amendments to the Immigration and Nationality Act abolish the nation-origin quotas and establish an annual limitation of 170,000 visas for immigrants in the eastern hemisphere.
1968	A limit is set for 120,000 immigrants annually from the western hemisphere.
1977	An amendment to the Immigration and Nationality Act abolishes separate quotas by hemisphere, changing the quota to 290,000 immigrants worldwide annually, with a limit of 20,000 for any one country.
1980	The Refugees Act reduces the worldwide quota to 270,000 immigrants.
1986	The Immigration Reform and Control Act allows those who have resided in the United States continuously since January 1, 1982, to apply for legal status and prohibits employers from hiring undocumented workers.
1990	The Immigration Act sets an annual ceiling of 700,000 immigrants per year to enter the United States for three years and an annual ceiling of 675,000 per year for every year after that.
1996	The Illegal Immigration Reform and Immigrant Responsibility Act makes it easier to deport aliens attempting to enter the United States without proper documents.

Who is a U.S. national?

A person is a U.S. national if she or he was born in American Samoa or Swains Island or is a descendant of a U.S. national. Previously, those born in Guam, Puerto Rico and the U.S. Virgin Islands were nationals, but they are now counted as citizens.

FACT:
Not all U.S. nationals are U.S. citizens.

Nationals who are not citizens cannot vote in national elections or hold elected national office. However, they may reside and work in the United States without restrictions and apply for citizenship under the same rules as other resident aliens.

Not all U.S. nationals are U.S. citizens; however, all U.S. citizens are U.S. nationals. U.S. passports normally make no distinction between the two and show only the bearer's nationality, not citizenship.

What documents does a U.S. citizen need to leave and then return to the United States?

In most cases, if a U.S. citizen is leaving the country and planning to reenter, a valid passport or passport card is required. There are some exceptions, such as when a cruise ship departs and returns to the same port (although a person without a passport might not be able to disembark at certain stops). Military personnel may travel without a passport, depending on the circumstances, and a child under the age of sixteen may travel to Mexico or Canada without a passport or passport card, if traveling with a parent. If a person is a lawful permanent resident (LPR), they must show their green card to reenter the United States.

Why do so few Americans have passports?

According to the State Department, as of 2012 there are 113,431,943 current passports in circulation, a record number and nearly one-third of U.S. citizens. Applying for a passport if you have never had one before currently costs $110 plus a $25 processing fee; renewing a passport costs $110. Passport applications and processing are available at many post offices; it takes an average of four to six weeks to receive a passport once you apply. To find out more about applying for a passport go to http://passports.state.gov.

What is a passport card?

The U.S. passport card is just a card, not a book, so it is more convenient and less expensive ($30) than a passport book. It can be used to enter the United States from Canada, Mexico, the Caribbean and Bermuda at land border crossings or sea ports of entry. The passport card cannot be used for international travel by air.

What is the Global Entry Program?

The Global Entry Program (GEP) expedites the screening and processing of low-risk, international travelers entering the United States. It is available for citizens, nationals and lawful permanent residents (LPRs) of the United States and some other countries, and uses biometric technology to verify, identity and confirm a person's status. Instead of standing in immigration processing lines when arriving into the United States, a GEP member swipes his or her passport or green card and then has a fingerprint scan and photo recorded.

A Global Entry Kiosk for entering the United States.

How can we be sure terrorists aren't entering our country?

Unlike some countries, the United States does not have an extensive profiling system and will not detain people legally entering the country if they have no criminal or suspicious background. All nineteen of the people who took part in the attack on the United States on September 11, 2001, entered the country on legal visas; only two of the nineteen were not fully legal at the time of the attack. All nineteen were well educated, from middle-class families, and had no criminal record and no known connection to terrorism. There would have been no reason to deny them entry then, and under the current immigration system they would still qualify to enter the United States.

In the case of the 2013 Boston Marathon bombing, Dzhokhar and Tamerlan Tsarnaev entered the United

States legally with their parents and obtained legal resident status. Dzhokhar became a naturalized U.S. citizen, while Tamerlan reportedly had a green card that allowed him to live and work legally in the United States, as well as leave and reenter the country. He was married to a U.S. citizen.

All in all, there is no evidence that there is a link between illegal immigration and terrorism. Those who want to do harm to the United States can most likely find a way to enter the country legally. However, some members of Congress have speculated that the Canadian border is particularly vulnerable to being crossed by potential terrorists and have called for more security along the Canadian border.

A U.S. border patrol agent surveys the Canadian border.

An Interior Department officer views the border fence with Mexico.

4. Major Issues Affecting U.S. Immigration

With all the talk about immigration, it is sometimes difficult to untangle the basic issues. In this chapter we look at three primary immigration issues facing the United States:

1. People living in the country without legal status.

2. Border security.

3. Improving legal immigration rules.

Does anyone really know how many people are living in the United States illegally?

A Pew study released in September 2013 estimates that 11.7 million people are living in the United States without legal status.[1] The study seems to show that unauthorized immigration has possibly increased from earlier estimates.

Although the Pew Research figures are generally accepted as a good estimate, other studies have concluded that the range could be between 7 million and 20 million people, since individuals without documentation tend not to fill out census forms or answer surveys, especially about their immigration status.

If someone is in the United States without legal status, isn't that person a criminal?

Being in the United States without documentation is a civil—not a criminal—offense, so under federal law, individuals living in the United States without proper documentation are not classified as criminals. The punishment may be deportation, but unless the person has committed a crime, he or she is not subject to criminal punishment.

Are undocumented immigrants more likely to commit crimes?

Most immigrants come to the United States to pursue economic and educational opportunities not available in their home countries and to build better lives for themselves and their families. Undocumented immigrants in particular have even more reason to not run afoul of the law given the risk of deportation that their lack of legal status entails.[2]

A number of studies show that immigrants generally have a lower level of criminal activity and incarceration than the general population, even when income and education levels are considered.[3]

A warning sign at the U.S. border.

If I know someone is in the United States illegally, do I need to report the person?

A U.S. citizen is under no obligation to report a person known or believed to be residing illegally in the United States. In fact, making such a report may put you in legal jeopardy. Although some websites now encourage such reports, the Immigration and Customs Enforcement Agency (ICE) primarily follows up on cases involving criminal activity (such as trafficking in persons) or an employer who is regularly hiring a number of people without documentation.

Why do we do so much to protect the rights of those in the United States illegally?

Although being a U.S. citizen offers certain rights and privileges, simply residing in the United States— legally or not—provides a person with a variety of protections not found in many other countries. These rights are guaranteed under "the equal protection act," or section 1 of the Fourteenth Amendment. While originally written to protect the rights of freed slaves, over the years court rulings have extended the protections to any minority group.

The Fourteenth Amendment to the Constitution

Section 1. All persons born or naturalized in the United States, and subject to the jurisdiction thereof, are citizens of the United States and of the State wherein they reside. No State shall make or enforce any law which shall abridge the privileges or immunities of citizens of the United States; nor shall any State deprive any person of life, liberty, or property, without due process of law; nor deny to any person within its jurisdiction the equal protection of the laws.

Why doesn't the United States deport everyone found in the country without documentation?

FACT:
The cost of deporting undocumented immigrants would be approximately $285 billion.

With an estimated 11 to 12 million people in the United States without legal status it is just not economically feasible to consider deporting everyone. The deputy director of Immigration and Customs Enforcement (ICE) told Congress that it costs about $12,500 to deport an undocumented immigrant, but a 2010 study by the Center for American Progress analyzed the ICE budget and estimated the cost at $23,480 per person.[4] This would mean the cost of massive deportation could be $285 billion—more than twice what the federal government spends in a year on education.

Morally, deporting many people would mean families would be separated, and in some cases, children born in the United States who are American citizens would potentially be separated from their parents who are not citizens. Many undocumented individuals have lived most of their lives in the United States and are responsible for the support of children, elderly relatives and others. Economists say some sectors of the economy would suffer greatly and even collapse without undocumented workers.

Then why are people deported?

About half of the people deported annually have been convicted of a crime and are then deported. In fiscal year 2011, 396,906 people were deported (the highest number of deportations ever) and 216,698 had been convicted of crimes, including:

- 44,653 convicted of "drug-related crimes"
- 35,927 convicted of driving under the influence
- 5,848 convicted of sexual offenses
- 1,119 convicted of homicide[5]

The rest have come to the attention of ICE through routine traffic stops, using forged documents, or as part of a crackdown on employers who hire undocumented workers. Some people are simply in the wrong place at the wrong time and are caught up in sweeps targeting others.

FACT:
In 2011, 396,906 people were deported, the largest number in any year.

What happens to children whose parents are deported?

According to the Shattered Families Report, of the 396,906 persons deported in 2011, 22 percent were the parents of children who are American citizens. More than 5,000 of those American citizen children have been placed in foster care as a result of deportations.[6] Individuals who have been deported have almost no ability to petition for parental rights or to be reunited with their children unless those children are able to return to the parent's country. Some children have even been put up for adoption when state courts have ruled that they were abandoned by their parents as a result of deportation.

Although current guidelines call for making exceptions to deportation for parents of young children, many of the people being deported do not speak English and lack legal representation, making it difficult for them to make a case for staying in the United States.

FACT:
States can determine eligibility for documents such as a driver's license.

Can states pass laws relating to immigrants?

Yes, states have the right to pass some laws relating to immigrants, such as eligibility for state-issued documents (including driver's licenses) and in-state tuition. For example, in fourteen states undocumented students qualify for in-state college tuition as long as they meet certain requirements.

Advertisement for driver's licenses and ID cards in Maryland.

The best-known example of a state law affecting immigrants was passed in Arizona in 2010. Called the "Support Our Law Enforcement and Safe Neighborhoods Act" but mostly known as SB 1070, the law required state police to determine an individual's immigration status during a "lawful stop, detention or arrest" and prohibited hiring, sheltering or transporting an unregistered immigrant. Although the Supreme Court ruled that some provisions of the law could not be enforced, it upheld the basic provision that allows police to determine a person's immigration status during a lawful stop.

> "Remember, remember always, that all of us ... are descended from immigrants and revolutionists."
>
> U.S. President Franklin D. Roosevelt

Do states determine who will be deported?

No, the federal government is responsible for deportations. Guidelines issued by the director of ICE in 2011 to agents, field offices and attorneys provide a list of factors to consider in determining if a person will be deported, including whether the person has any criminal history, if he or she has pursued an education and has family members in the United States, whether the person is a primary caretaker for a dependent, and how the person came to the United States and at what age. Because of the cost of deportations and limited resources, the highest priority for deportation continues to be those involved in criminal activity, especially related to drug or human trafficking.

Can a person with a green card be deported?

A person with a green card is a lawful permanent resident (LPR) of the United States and is entitled to many of the benefits of citizenship. However, especially within the first five years of receiving LPR status, a person can be deported if he or she is convicted of certain crimes. The only protection against deportation is to become a U.S. citizen.

What is self-deportation?

Self-deportation means that if conditions become difficult enough, immigrants may choose to leave and return to their country of origin. In states such as Arizona where laws have become increasingly dif-

MCGR
SUR

xxxxxxx0309

2/22/2022

Item: ï¿½00100840085231 ((book)

ficult for immigrants, "attrition through enforcement" is a similar concept, meaning those without documentation will leave rather than face the increasingly hostile legal environment.

What is DACA?

Implemented by the executive branch in August 2012, the Deferred Action for Childhood Arrivals (DACA) program allows individuals who meet certain guidelines to request approval to be protected from deportation for a period of two years, subject to renewal, and to possibly be eligible for employment authorization. Previous proposed legislation was called the Development, Relief and Education for Alien Minors Act (DREAM Act), and those who qualify under DACA

Young people rally for the DREAM Act.

are often called DREAMers. Although the status does not grant long-term immigration status, it does protect the DREAMers until the immigration laws are changed. An estimated 900,000 individuals were eligible when the program was announced.

Who is eligible for DACA?

Individuals who:

1. Were under the age of thirty-one as of June 15, 2012;
2. Came to the United States before reaching their sixteenth birthday;
3. Have continuously resided in the United States since June 15, 2007, up to the present time;
4. Were physically present in the United States on June 15, 2012, and at the time of making the request for consideration of deferred action with USCIS;
5. Entered without inspection before June 15, 2012, or lawful immigration status expired as of June 15, 2012;
6. Are currently in school, have graduated or obtained a certificate of completion from high school, have obtained a general education development (GED) certificate, or are an honorably discharged veteran of the Coast Guard or Armed Forces of the United States; and
7. Have not been convicted of a felony, significant misdemeanor, three or more other misdemeanors, and do not otherwise pose a threat to national security or public safety.

Do people continue to enter the United States by crossing our borders?

According to a recent study, in 2012, 365,000 people were caught trying to cross into the United States from Mexico. Estimates are that a nearly equal number of people succeeded, according to a *Washington Post* story.[7] Along the Canadian border, the number is much lower, with 7,431 caught in 2010.[8]

How does security compare between the U.S.-Mexican border and the U.S.-Canadian border?

The U.S. border with Canada is 5,525 miles long, the longest international border in the world and often called the longest undefended border in the world. The U.S. border with Mexico is approximately one-third the length. Although the border with Canada is much longer, the volume of people crossing is lower and far fewer people attempt to cross at unregulated border crossings. Canadian and U.S. border agents and officers both patrol the border and generally share information and coordinate security. Trade between the United States and Canada is significant, so border crossings balance the need for security with the importance of encouraging commerce. Still, the border with Canada is mostly unpatrolled and some studies show that it represents a greater threat from terrorists.

FACT:
The U.S. border with Canada is 5,525 miles long.

The U.S. border with Mexico has much higher volume, especially of individuals, so the challenge is to balance security with tourism, a significant source of revenue for both countries. U.S. funding to Mexico is helping build up the patrol on the Mexican side of the border, but in general, Mexican border patrol is less robust than in Canada. Adding more security measures to the Mexican border at crossing points would potentially back up traffic for

Border sign.

hours and cut down on tourism as well as hurt the many people who legally cross the border daily to work.

What needs to be done to improve border security between the United States and Mexico?

There are differing opinions on what needs to be done to improve security, with some studies claiming there need to be substantially more border patrol agents and others saying there simply needs to be more coordination between the various agencies patrolling the border.

Some proposed legislation calls for more fencing on the border and enhanced border patrols and surveillance. Some suggest enforcing punishment for those caught attempting to cross the border (instead of simply sending them back) since most people who cross into the United States have made multiple attempts.

The Merida Initiative, launched in 2008, is a program to improve cooperation between the United States and Mexico in order to enhance border security and combat the drug violence that has plagued Mexico.

How often are drugs brought across the border from Mexico?

Getting drugs from Mexico into the United States is big business, and Mexican cartels spare little expense or

A tunnel used to smuggle drugs from Mexico into the United States.

violence to accomplish their mission. One estimate puts the annual value of drugs trafficked into the United States from Mexico at $39 billion.[9]

Drugs are smuggled into the United States through tunnels, by air, and via every possible vehicle or person entering the country. Individuals with visas to cross the border regularly for work or school are often targeted by drug cartels and become "mules" who carry drugs over the border, often because their families are threatened or even kidnapped. American tourists have even been targeted and have sometimes discovered that drugs have been placed in their cars in order to smuggle them across the border.

What's wrong with the current U.S. immigration system?

The current U.S. immigration system is neither comprehensive nor internally consistent, creating confusion and inconsistencies for those who want to legally enter the United States. Some lawmakers contend that the problems with the current system actually help encourage illegal immigration since in some cases it is more difficult to navigate the legal system than to enter the country illegally or overstay a visa.

Most experts agree that the current system is too complex, creating too much red tape and making it difficult to unite families, offer employment opportunities to highly qualified workers and offer well-educated students the chance to stay in the United States after completing their degrees.

How many people are "in line" to enter the United States legally?

An estimated 4.5 million people are currently waiting to have their visa applications processed in order to enter the United States legally. Some have been waiting more than two decades to enter the country based on their family status and country of origin.[10] For example, people from Mexico or the Philippines may wait more than fifteen years to have their visa processed while those from other countries may wait a year or two. Individuals attempting to enter because of work may be processed immediately. Immigration lawyers contend that the processing system is inefficient and even contradictory with a combination of preferences and maximum quotas. More than 1.3 million Mexicans are waiting for a family preference visa, with the 2013 maximum visa allowance per country set at just 15,820.[11]

Doesn't a quota system discriminate against certain groups of people?

The U.S. immigration system has included quotas since 1924 as a way to provide for a diverse pool of immigrants to enter the country. The strict quota system was abolished in 1965, but there are still caps on the number of visas issued in different categories that essentially create quotas.

As long as the United States has an annual cap on the total number of immigrants, there needs to be a way to give a somewhat equal opportunity to people from any country who want to move to the United States, while still attempting to unite families and provide for the needs of society, including certain types of workers. Capping the number of visas issued per country is not viewed as a quota system per se, but by applying the same percentage of total visas available to all countries, regardless of population, some countries will almost always have more visa applications than are available. Under this system, countries like Mexico, the Philippines, China and India always have more applicants than visas available, while countries with small populations may not use the visas available to them.

July 23, 1892

CHINESE?

NO! NO! NO!

Come to 10th and A Streets at 7:30 Monday evening and express your opinion on the Chinese question.

SHALL WE HAVE

CHINESE

NO! NO! NO!

Image courtesy of the
Washington State Historical Society, Tacoma

An 1892 poster for a rally to exclude Chinese immigrants.

What is meant by "anchor babies"?

"Anchor baby" is considered a pejorative term for babies born in the United States to mothers who do not have legal status themselves. However, it is also used to describe babies born to so-called "birth tourists" or women who enter the United States legally as tourists while pregnant and have their babies on American soil before returning to their home. Because of birthright citizenship, the child automatically becomes a U.S. citizen. Birth tourism has become big business, and firms advertise openly, especially in Asian countries. "Some of the websites blatantly advertise the advantages of free public school in America, a chance to get grants to colleges like Harvard and Yale, and an easier path for the whole family to get green cards once the child turns 21," according to a recent report on NBC's *Rock Center*.[12]

While some members of Congress have made attempts to block the practice, it is not illegal for a pregnant woman to enter the United States on a tourist visa.

Why have churches and religious leaders become involved in the immigration issue?

Many religious institutions have been on the frontlines of the immigration battle as members of their

congregations faced discrimination and potential deportation. According to a 2012 statement by the Evangelical Immigration Table, "Our national immigration laws have created a moral, economic and political crisis in America."[13]

Many spiritual leaders view the current immigration crisis as a moral issue, citing Scripture verses about "welcoming the stranger" and noting biblical examples of hospitality and kindness to those who are from another land.

Of the approved organizations that resettle refugees in the United States, most are religious groups and have had a long history of involving their congregations in work with immigrants. Hispanic immigrants, especially, are responsible for the growth in many Catholic and evangelical congregations and have become a strong voice within religious circles.

"Do not forget to entertain strangers, for by so doing some have unwittingly entertained angels."

Hebrew 13:2
NKJV

A union marches for immigration reform.

5. Economics of Immigration

Do immigrants drain the economy or boost it? There are strong feelings on both sides of the argument. Here are some of the basic economic facts.

How do immigrants help the economy?

The debate over the economic impact of immigrants has raged since groups of foreign-born workers first began coming to the United States. For the most part, immigrants have been highly productive members of U.S. society and the U.S. economy. According to the Small Business Administration (SBA), 18 percent of all U.S. small business owners are immigrants, and the Fiscal Policy Institute estimates that immigrant-owned small businesses generate more than $776 billion annually.[1]

According to the National Venture Capital Association, immigrants have started 25 percent of public U.S. companies that then received backing by venture capital investors, including Google, eBay, Yahoo!, Sun Microsystems and Intel.[2] Of the companies on the Fortune 500 list, 40 percent were founded by an immigrant or the child of an immigrant.[3]

In addition to creating companies and jobs at the highest level, immigrants also make up a large share of workers at the lowest levels of the U.S. economy. Foreign-born workers make up a fairly large percentage of workers in service industries, construction and agriculture. Many businesses rely on the availability of these workers and are concerned that any move to restrict immigration would make it difficult to keep their businesses afloat.

For the most part, almost all sectors of the business community support immigration reform that includes a pathway to citizenship for those in the country, a guest worker program and new visa categories that increase the opportunities to bring highly skilled workers into the country.

Why do people feel that immigrants hurt business?

FACT:
Immigrants make up a large percentage of workers in service industries.

Undocumented workers are sometimes hired by employers who pay less than minimum wage, potentially driving down the cost to the employer as well as the pay scale for other employees. Some work "off the books" either on a cash basis or as contractors and don't pay taxes or have them withheld from their wages. They are consumers, but many send a percentage of their income back to their home country in remittances. Children (whether documented or not) attend public schools, and anyone who arrives at a hospital needing emergency care receives it, whatever their immigration status.

According to Jack Martin, director of special projects for the Federation for Immigration Reform (FAIR), undocumented immigrants cost federal and state governments an estimated $10.7 billion a year in health care spending. This figure includes the cost of babies born to undocumented immigrant parents without insurance in U.S. hospitals, at taxpayers' expense or at the expense of the hospital.[4]

The cost of public schooling for children who are undocumented (or whose parents are) is more difficult to estimate, since they are mostly state costs. But one source estimates a national total funding cost of $44.5 billion annually.[5]

Google cofounder Sergey Brin is a Russian immigrant.

Do immigrants pay taxes?

People who live in the United States pay sales taxes on everything they purchase, regardless of their status. Undocumented immigrants are also responsible for taxes assessed on their personal property. Some pay income tax as well.

Some immigrants in the United States who are not lawful permanent residents obtain Social Security Numbers and pay taxes; others obtain Individual Taxpayer Identification Numbers (ITINs) and pay taxes from their wages.

Some workers in the United States use forged or illegally obtained documents to get a job. Their employer withholds taxes from their wages even though that worker will not file for a refund or use Social Security or Medicare, benefits funded by individual workers' income taxes.

What happens to funds withheld from paychecks of undocumented workers?

Workers whose paychecks have taxes and Social Security payments withheld under numbers that don't match their names simply lose access to the funds, which go to the Social Security trust fund.

According to Stephen Goss, chief actuary for the Social Security Administration, 3.1 million workers without legal documents pay into Social Security each year. In 2010, these workers and their employers paid $15 billion to Social Security, although they will have almost no chance to claim the benefits.

As much as $150 billion of undocumented workers' money has flowed into the Social Security trust fund, or about 8 percent of the total money Social Security has in reserve ($1.7 trillion).[6]

What is an ITIN?

An ITIN, or Individual Taxpayer Identification Number, is a nine-digit tax processing number issued by the IRS to certain non-resident and resident aliens,

Tijuana–San Diego border.

their spouses and their dependents who do not have or
cannot obtain a Social Security Number (SSN). Beginning with the number 9, it is formatted like a Social
Security Number (9##-##-####). The number cannot
be used to prove identity or obtain benefits.

Applicants are not required to apply for an ITIN in
person and may obtain one while still living abroad. The
Internal Revenue Service (IRS) does not validate the authenticity of identity documents used to obtain the ITIN.
According to the IRS, "ITINs do not prove identity
outside the Federal tax system, and should not be offered
or accepted as identification for non-tax purposes."[7]

What are remittances?

When a foreign-born worker transfers funds back to his
or her home country (often to support the worker's extended family), it is called a *remittance*. The World Bank
estimates that in 2012, overall global remittances to
poor countries were more than $400 billion. This is

almost equal to the total amount of foreign direct investment. The top recipients of remittances in 2012 were India ($70 billion), China ($66 billion), the Philippines ($24 billion), Mexico ($24 billion) and Nigeria ($21 billion).[8] The top sending country was the United States.

Remittances are subject to a transfer fee as well as a fee to convert the funds into local currency. These fees are not regulated, but because of recent legislation, they must be disclosed. Because poor workers are often sending small amounts at a time, the fees make up a high percentage.

Photo by FutureAtlas.com.

How do immigrants send money home?

In addition to physically carrying money in suitcases and on their person, immigrants send money home via companies like MoneyGram and Western Union.

According to a recent article in the *Economist*, "Western Union is the gorilla of money transfers, handling close to $1 in every $5 that is wired around the world."[9]

In 2012, the Western Union Company completed 231 million consumer-to-consumer transactions worldwide valued at $79 billion.[10]

Who is eligible to receive food stamps?

Food stamps (now called SNAP—Supplemental Nutrition Assistance Program) provide financial assistance for purchasing food to low- or no-income people living in the United States. Administered by the U.S. Department of Agriculture (USDA), the benefits are distributed by states and are primarily available to U.S. citizens and lawful permanent residents. However, some non-citizens are eligible if they are refugees or victims of human trafficking, or if they meet certain other qualifications. Most programs assign an electronic debit card that can be used to purchase prepackaged food from participating grocery stores but not food from delis or fast food restaurants.

We Accept

SNAP

BENEFITS

This institution is an equal opportunity provider.
U.S. Department of Agriculture
Food and Nutrition Service
FNS 132 • Revised December 2008

In many immigrant households, children are U.S. citizens but parents are not. The USDA checks the status people who will receive SNAP benefits, not the person applying on their behalf. If the adults in a household are not documented, their income is not considered in eligibility requirements, and therefore the children often qualify to receive SNAP.

What is WIC? Are undocumented immigrants eligible?

WIC is the U.S. Department of Agriculture's Special Supplemental Nutrition Program for Women, Infants and Children. It provides grants to states to safeguard the health of low-income pregnant, postpartum and breastfeeding women, infants and children up to age five. In most cases a person does not have to hold legal resident status in order to qualify to receive benefits.

Can undocumented immigrants buy health insurance?

Most people in the United States receive their health insurance coverage through an employer plan. But for undocumented workers, insurance is often unavailable through an employer and must be bought at a much higher individual rate, making the cost prohibitive. The Affordable Care Act provides U.S. government subsidies only to those buying insurance who can prove their legal status and does not allow undocumented individuals to apply for Medicaid or to use the state insurance exchanges. Because of this, most undocumented immigrants will remain uninsured.

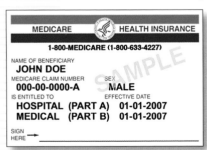

Non-citizens are not entitled to Medicare Part A but may purchase Part B under certain conditions.

Does a hospital have to treat someone without documentation?

The Emergency Medical Treatment and Active Labor Act (EMTALA) requires hospitals to provide care to anyone needing emergency healthcare treatment, regardless of citizenship, legal status or ability to pay. Hospitals may only transfer or discharge patients needing emergency treatment with their own informed consent, after stabilization or when their condition requires transfer to a hospital better equipped to administer the treatment. In some places the cost of emergency treatment has bankrupted hospitals or caused them to close their emergency rooms. However, many of the EMTALA provisions apply to a health facility even if it does not have an emergency room.

Hospitals do not have to provide care to those who are stabilized but may be dealing with chronic or long-term health conditions, so most undocumented immigrants receive little or no health care except through community clinics.

FACT:
All children, including undocumented children, are required to attend school.

Do immigrant children have the right to attend public school?

Not only do undocumented children have the right to attend school, they are actually obligated under state laws to attend school until they reach a certain age. A 1982 U.S. Supreme Court ruling determined that public schools could not deny admission or treat a student differently because of immigration status. The ruling also stated that teachers and school officials could not make inquiries of students or parents that might reveal their immigration status, nor could they require Social Security Numbers from students, since doing so would expose a person's status. The ruling also explicitly stated that school personnel were not obligated to inform anyone if a person's undocumented status was revealed.

Are undocumented students allowed to attend college or university?

Most colleges and universities are open to all students. Fourteen states extend in-state college tuition rates to students who are undocumented but attended high school in the state and meet other requirements. Federal aid and loans are generally not available to students who are not citizens, lawful permanent residents or refugees.

Are foreign students allowed to work in the United States while attending school?

Most foreign students enter the United States on an F-1 (student) or J-1 (exchange visitor) visa. Under the provisions of those visas, in addition to being enrolled in an academic program, a student may be employed up to twenty hours per week during the academic year and up to forty hours per week during summers and vacations. Internships and other "practical training" jobs are also allowed under these visas. Students in the United States without documentation sometimes work as consultants or take cash jobs such as house cleaning, babysitting or yard work.

Can foreign or undocumented students obtain U.S. Social Security cards?

Students with valid F-1 student visas who are enrolled full time in an academic institution and are working may obtain Social Security cards.

Can non-citizens receive Medicare?

American citizens are automatically enrolled in Part A and Part B of Medicare at the age of sixty-five. If they have paid taxes, they receive Part A coverage for free. Non-citizens are not entitled to Part A but may purchase Part B (medical insurance) if they are sixty-five years of age or older and were legally admitted to the United States, and if their status is still legal when they apply. They also must have lived in the United States for at least five consecutive years.

Medicare Part D helps cover prescription drugs and requires a monthly premium payment. Anyone who has Part A or B can also purchase Part D. Premiums are set depending on income level.

FACT:
Students in the United States on a student visa are permitted to work and obtain a Social Security card.

What about Medicaid?

States determine who is eligible for Medicaid, but more than half of the states provide Medicaid to children and pregnant women who are immigrants and may not be lawful permanent residents. Under the Affordable Care Act, only those with legal status in the United States will be eligible for Medicaid.

Could I get in trouble if I hire someone to do odd jobs and then find out the person isn't documented?

If someone is working as an independent contractor, you are not obligated to confirm their work authorization. You can be held liable, however, if you hire an independent contractor knowing that they are not authorized to work in the United States.

Can I ask a person if he or she is a citizen during an interview?

You cannot ask anything about a person's immigration status during an interview or at any time before the person is actually hired. The Immigration Reform and

Control Act of 1986 (IRCA) makes it illegal for employers to discriminate in hiring, firing or recruiting based on an individual's immigration status. The law also prohibits employers from rejecting valid documents or insisting on additional documents (beyond what is legally required for Form I-9, which confirms the employee's identity). As long as a document appears genuine, an employer may not question its authenticity.

While employers are not allowed to ask job applicants any questions relating to status or documentation, once a formal offer has been made employers must verify the new employee's identity and employment eligibility. An employer is allowed to include the following statement on job postings: "In compliance with federal law, all persons hired will be required to verify identity and eligibility to work in the United States and to complete the required employment eligibility verification document form upon hire."

FACT:
It is illegal to ask about a person's immigration status before offering them a job.

E-Verify allows businesses to determine work eligibility.

What is E-Verify?

Under U.S. law, companies must only employ individuals who may legally work in the United States, including citizens, lawful permanent residents (LPR) or foreign citizens with authorization. E-Verify is an online system that allows businesses to determine the work eligibility of their employees. Although the system is currently used by a minority of companies, state and federal authorities alike are considering making the use of E-Verify mandatory. An increasing number of businesses are posting the notice that they use E-Verify for screening employees, an indication that undocumented workers will not be eligible to work for the business.

What is an investor visa?

An investor visa (otherwise known as an EB-5 visa) is a special category of U.S. visa designed to encourage entrepreneurial activity and to bring business to the United States. There are 10,000 investor visas available each year.

To qualify for this type of visa, a businessperson must offer a business plan and either invest a substantial amount (at least $500,000) or prove that qualified investors are prepared to offer venture capital for the enterprise. The business plan must show that the business can create revenue and a certain number of jobs at a certain salary level, as well as other marks of the proposed business's viability. The visa allows the investor and immediate family members to obtain legal residency.

Why do businesses want more visas for highly skilled workers?

Many countries have immigration systems that encourage highly skilled workers to immigrate with a minimum of red tape. Many also allow students who have received advanced degrees, especially in areas such as science, engineering and technology, to apply for legal residence. The U.S. system requires students to leave the country once their education has ended and creates much greater obstacles for highly skilled workers. U.S. businesses believe this creates a "brain drain" that favors other countries and puts them at an unfair advantage in world markets.

An advertisement in South African Airways magazine for an investor visa.

6. Who Are the Immigrants?

Currently, immigrants make up 13 percent of the U.S. population. Here we explore who they are.

Who are immigrants in America today?

The term *immigrant* refers to a wide range of people. Some have lived in the United States for many years and have become citizens. The 18 million people in this group may seem very "American," although technically they are immigrants or "foreign born." Well-known Americans in this category include former Secretary of State Madeleine Albright (born in Czechoslovakia) and singer Neil Young (born in Canada).

Another group of immigrants is made up of lawful permanent residents, those 13 million people who hold "green cards." While they are not citizens, they have the right to work and receive benefits and most other privileges of a U.S. citizen. Singer Rihanna (a citizen of Barbados) is in this category.

Refugees and asylum seekers are also legal immigrants. Actor Andy Garcia (whose family fled Cuba) and singer Wyclef Jean (a refugee from Haiti) are examples of immigrants who entered the United States as refugees.

Immigrants who entered the United States illegally or who entered legally but overstayed their visas are "undocumented immigrants" or "immigrants without status." Actress Salma Hayek has told various sources that for a period of time when her visa had expired, she was "an illegal immigrant in the US."[1]

Do certain cultural traits make some immigrants more successful than others?

In 2013 a controversial book, *The Triple Package* by Amy Chu and Jed Rubenfeld, hypothesized that some immigrant groups, including Cubans, Iranians, Nigerians, and some Indians and Asians, experienced upward mobility in the United States at higher rates because they possess certain cultural qualities.

Actress Natalie Portman is an immigrant from Israel.

Critics of the book say that it ignores the history of each group's arrival, including the fact that some groups (like Cubans) had their immigration supported and facilitated by the U.S. government, and others arrived with advanced degrees and the ability to speak English or came to the U.S. primarily to earn advanced degrees. Some groups brought wealth with them (such as Cubans and Iranians) and were able to continue businesses that had already made them wealthy.

Some supporters of immigration reform point out that all immigrant groups benefit from access to better education and are better assimilated if they can speak English.

Does the United States have room for so many immigrants?

The United States is the third-largest country in the world, with an estimated 2012 population of 313,914,000, according to the U.S. Census Bureau. With more than 80 percent of the population living in cities and suburbs, vast amounts of U.S. land remain unpopulated. So there is plenty of space for immigrants. The greater issue is how they assimilate and whether U.S. social systems can support the growing population.

FACT:
Immigrants make up 13 percent of the U.S. population.

Why does it seem that there are more and more immigrants every year?

As a total number, there are more immigrants than ever before, but as a percentage, they make up about 13 percent of the population, which is not unprecedented. The first U.S. census to collect information on place of birth was in 1850, when foreign-born persons made up almost 10 percent of the total population. Between 1860 and 1920, immigrants as a percentage of the population ranged from 13 to 15 percent. By 1930, immigrants were less than 12 percent.

With legislation capping immigration numbers, the percentage declined until 1970, when it reached a record low of 5 percent of the total population. Since then, the percentage has increased, rising to 8 percent in 1990, 11 percent in 2000, and 13 percent as of the 2010 census. So, over the last four decades, most adult Americans have witnessed a rapid increase in immigrants both in total number and by percentage. Although the percentage isn't unprecedented, the total numbers are higher, and the increase more rapid, than any time in history.

What determines how many immigrants enter the United States each year?

The number of legal immigrations to the United States is almost entirely dependent on U.S. immigration policy, since there are always more people who want to immigrate than there are openings under the various

"A simple way to take measure of a country is to look at how many want in and how many want out."

Tony Blair

Place of Birth of Immigrants in the United States—Top Ten Countries

Top Ten Countries	2010	2000	1990
Mexico	11,711,103	9,177,487	4,298,014
China	2,166,526	1,518,652	921,070
India	1,780,322	1,022,552	450,406
Philippines	1,777,588	1,369,070	912,674
Vietnam	1,240,542	988,174	543,262
El Salvador	1,214,049	817,336	465,433
Cuba	1,104,679	872,716	736,971
South Korea	1,100,422	864,125	568,397
Dominican Republic	879,187	687,677	347,858
Guatemala	830,824	480,665	225,739

Source: 1990 and 2000 Decennial Census and 2010 American Community Survey.

quotas or limits. In the 1950s, immigration was capped at 250,000 persons annually. By 2000, because of the change in immigration laws and quotas, legal immigration had risen to more than 1 million each year. (In 1990, legal immigrations spiked to nearly 2 million because of the 1986 Immigration Reform and Control Act that granted legal status to nearly 3 million immigrants through its passage and subsequent additions.)

What is the racial makeup of Americans?

According to the U.S. Census Bureau, 72 percent of Americans are white, 13 percent are African American, 5 percent are Asian, and 16 percent self-identify as Hispanic or Latino. These numbers are based on the way individuals define themselves, and do not necessarily track with other studies.

FACT:
Of the U.S. population, 72 percent self-identify as "white."

Where are most recent immigrants coming from?

Nearly 11.7 million people born in Mexico now reside in the United States, according to the 2010 American Community Survey. Mexican immigrants accounted for 29 percent of all immigrants in the United States in 2010.

How many U.S. residents are Hispanic and have legal status?

In 2012, more than 53 million residents identified themselves as Hispanic or Latino, according to the U.S. Census Bureau. The majority of them are citizens, having been born in the U.S. (approximately 34 million), with another 12 million either becoming naturalized citizens or residing as legal residents.

Of the estimated 11.7 undocumented residents of the United States, the Pew Research Center estimates that approximately 9 million are Hispanic (mostly Mexican). So of the total number of Hispanic residents in the United States, a minority—approximately one in six—lacks legal status.

Of the total foreign-born population in the United States, nearly half are of Hispanic or Latino origin, based on the 2010 U.S. Census. These statistics are drawn from different sources and often rely on self-identification.

Percent of Immigrant Population by State

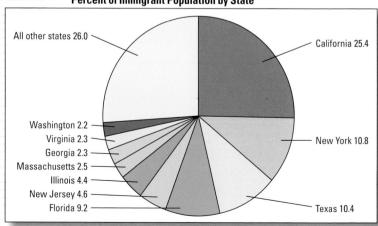

All other states 26.0

California 25.4

Washington 2.2
Virginia 2.3
Georgia 2.3
Massachusetts 2.5
Illinois 4.4
New Jersey 4.6
Florida 9.2

New York 10.8

Texas 10.4

In which states do most immigrants live?

California has the largest foreign-born population, with more than one in four residents foreign born, followed by New York with 11 percent, Texas with 10 percent, Florida with 9 percent, then New Jersey and Illinois each with around 4 percent.

Do most legal immigrants become citizens?

According to the U.S. Census Bureau, a little more than half of all immigrants actually become citizens. The percentage is lower among Hispanics and lowest among those legal immigrants from Mexico, with only 36 percent becoming citizens, according to the Pew Research Center.

This statistic is often cited by proponents of immigration reform who advocate a reduction in deportations without a pathway to full citizenship. This position contends that most of those immigrants who are

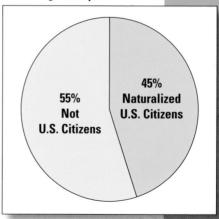

U.S. Immigrant Population

55% Not U.S. Citizens

45% Naturalized U.S. Citizens

Source: 2011 American Community Survey, U.S. Census Bureau.

in the United States illegally will never seek citizenship anyway, based on this data.

Becoming a legal permanent resident (LPR) of the United States provides most of the benefits of citizenship and removes most of the threat of deportation.

How many Mexican-born workers are in the U.S. labor force?

In 2010 approximately 70 percent of the 11 million immigrants from Mexico ages sixteen and older were in the civilian labor force, compared to 68 percent of the total immigrant population ages sixteen and older (37.7 million) and 63 percent of the 206.1 million native-born ages sixteen and older.

Countries by Immigrant Population

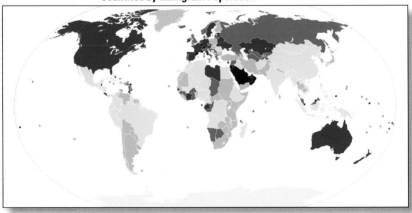

Black: more than 50% of the world's immigrants; dark blue: 20-50%; bright blue: 10-20%; light blue: less than 10%.

How many children who are citizens have parents without legal status?

An article in 2011 estimates that 4.5 million children who are U.S. citizens have at least one parent who lacks legal status in the United States.[2]

Who are most of the people entering illegally?

Although there are no accurate numbers, estimates are that 60 percent of those entering the United States illegally are from Mexico, another 23 percent from Latin America, 11 percent from Asia and 5 percent from Canada and Europe.

Why do people enter illegally?

The United States has a long border with Mexico, making effective border patrol difficult. And the economies of the two countries are very different, with the United States affording more opportunities and a better future for children. It can be tempting for people to cross into the United States, particularly given the promise of citizenship for any child born on U.S. soil.

But there is another reason people enter the United

States illegally. A large number of legal immigrants in the United States (both citizens and lawful permanent residents) are from Mexico, and many of them have family members who want to join them. The U.S. immigration system restricts the number of people from any one country who can legally enter the United States, so the wait for visas based on family relationship (especially from a country like Mexico) can be more than a decade. Even under the best proposals for immigration reform, with those who are illegally in the United States making restitution and entering the formal immigration process, such immigrants will have to "get in line" behind those who have already applied. According to the *Washington Post*, "Wait times . . . vary wildly depending on the green card that a prospective immigrant is applying for, the number of visas available and his or her country of origin."[3] A Mexican son or daughter of a naturalized U.S. citizen might have to wait twenty years to be processed for a green card; a child from the Philippines could be in line for fifteen years.

An *NBC News* report suggests the situation is even worse for relatives of lawful permanent residents. Sergio Garcia, a Mexican citizen, began the naturalization process in 1995 when he was seventeen, and his father, a lawful permanent resident of the United States, sponsored him. Originally he was told it would take three to five years before he could begin the process of getting a green card. But Garcia continues to wait; the latest estimate is that he will be eligible in 2019—nearly twenty-five years after beginning the process.[4]

Because of these types of stories, some families choose to reunite either by crossing the border illegally or obtaining visitor visas and then simply staying in the United States.

How many immigrants come to the United States as refugees?

Refugees are admitted to the United States based on an inability to return to their home countries because of a "well-founded fear of persecution" due to their race, membership in a social group, political opinion, religion or national origin. Refugees apply for admission from outside of the United States, generally from a "transition country" rather than their home country.

Each year the U.S. president, in consultation with Congress, determines the numerical ceiling for refugee admissions. The total limit is broken down further into regional limits. There are preference or priority categories for refugees based on the degree of risk they face, and whether or not they have family members in the United States, and every year the president and Congress designate certain groups as being of special concern to the United States. Applicants for refugee status who are members of those groups are given special consideration.

After September 11, 2001, the number of refugees admitted into the United States fell dramatically, but

> *"We live in the age of the refugee, the age of the exile."*
>
> Ariel Dorfman

Regional Limits for Refugee Admission to the United States, Fiscal Year 2010

Africa	15,500
East Asia	17,000
Europe and Central Asia	2,500
Latin America/Caribbean	5,000
Near East/South Asia	35,000
Unallocated Reserve	5,000
TOTAL	**80,000**

the numerical limits have been increased in the past several years.

For fiscal year 2010 the president announced that up to 80,000 refugees could be admitted to the United States.

How many people have sought asylum in the United States?

People who were persecuted in their home country, or who fear persecution upon their return, may apply for asylum in the United States. They must apply within one year of admission to the United States, or they may apply at a port of entry when they first seek admission. There is no limit on the number of individuals who may be granted asylum in a given year, nor are there specific categories for determining who may seek asylum. In 2010, 21,113 individuals were granted asylum, according to the U.S. Office of Immigration Statistics.[5] Like refugees, asylum seekers are eligible to become lawful permanent residents one year after admission to the United States as a refugee, or one year after being granted asylum.

How many people in the United States hold "temporary protected status"?

Temporary protected status (TPS) is granted to people who are in the United States but cannot return to their home country because of "natural disaster," "extraordinary temporary conditions" or "ongoing armed conflict." The status has been in effect for more than twenty years and includes as many as 300,000 people, some of whom have now lived in the United States "temporarily" for two decades. Because it is considered a temporary status, it does not offer a pathway to permanent residence or citizenship, leaving those who are protected by it also in limbo.[6]

FACT: As many as 300,000 people live in the United States under temporary protected status (TPS).

What is "deferred enforced departure"?

Deferred enforced departure (DED) provides protection from deportation for individuals whose home countries are unstable, therefore making return dangerous. Currently this status only applies to Liberians. It has been criticized because the Liberian civil war ended in 2003 and the country does not even have a State Department travel warning for U.S. citizens.

What is "humanitarian parole"?

Certain individuals may be allowed to enter the United States under humanitarian parole status even though they may not meet the definition of a refugee and may not be eligible to immigrate through other channels. Such status may be granted temporarily for urgent humanitarian reasons or significant public benefit.

Who are the unauthorized immigrants?

FACT:
*As of 2012,
there were an
estimated 11.7
unauthorized
immigrants
living in the
United States.*

The Pew Hispanic Center estimates that 11.7 million un-authorized immigrants lived in the United States in 2012. Unauthorized immigration peaked at 12 million in 2007; it has fallen since then mainly because of less immigration from Mexico, the largest source of U.S. immigrants. In 2010, unauthorized immigrants from Mexico made up 58 percent of all unauthorized immigrants.[7]

Nearly two-thirds of unauthorized immigrants in 2010 had lived in the United States for at least a decade; nearly half (46 percent) were parents of minor children. There were 1 million unauthorized immigrants under age eighteen in the United States, as well as 4.5 million U.S.-born children whose parents were unauthorized. An esti-mated 9 million people lived in "mixed-status" families.[8]

According to 2008 data, unauthorized immigrants make up 25 percent of farm workers (not including temporary workers).[9]

What share of all immigrants in the United States are women?

In 2010, approximately 51 percent of the immigrant pop-ulation was female. The share of women has fluctuated slightly in the past three decades. Women accounted for 53 percent of the 14.1 million immigrants in 1980, 51 percent of the 19.7 million immigrants in 1990, and 50 percent of the 31.1 million immigrants in 2000.

What is the age distribution of the immigrant population?

In 2010, less than 1 percent of the foreign-born population in the United States was under the age of five (compared to 7 percent of the native-born population); 6 percent were five to seventeen years old (compared to 19 percent native-born); 9 percent were aged eighteen to twenty-four (native-born: 10 percent); 72 percent were aged twenty-five to sixty-four (native-born: 50 percent); and 12 percent were sixty-five years of age or older (native-born: 13 percent). Overall the immigrant population in 2010 was older than the U.S.-born population; the median age of immigrants was 41.4 years, compared to 35.9 years among the native-born population.

How many immigrants have come to the United States since 2000?

Of the 40 million foreign-born people in the United States in 2010, 38 percent entered the country prior to 1990, 27 percent entered between 1990 and 1999, and almost 35 percent entered in 2000 or later.

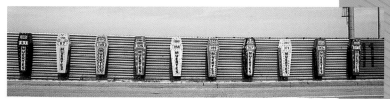

Mexican border death memorial.

How many immigrants are naturalized U.S. citizens?

Just over two in five (or almost 17.5 million) immigrants in the United States in 2010 were naturalized U.S. citizens. The remaining 56 percent of immigrants (or 22.5 million) included lawful permanent residents, unauthorized immigrants and legal residents on temporary visas, such as students and temporary workers. Of the 17.5 million naturalized citizens in 2010, 44 percent naturalized since 2000, 27 percent naturalized between 1990 and 1999, 14 percent naturalized between 1980 and 1989, and 15 percent naturalized prior to 1980.

Which languages does the U.S. population speak?

According to the U.S. Census, in 2010 approximately 79 percent of the U.S. population ages five and older stated that they speak only English at home. One in five people (59.5 million) reported speaking a language other than English—Spanish being by far the most common (62 percent), followed by "Chinese" (including Mandarin and Cantonese, almost 5 percent), Tagalog (almost 3 percent), Vietnamese (2 percent), "French" (including Cajun and Patois, 2 percent), Korean (almost 2 percent), German (almost 2 percent), Arabic (1 percent), and Russian (1 percent).

How many people in the United States speak only limited English?

In 2010 there were 25.2 million limited English proficient (LEP) individuals (people who reported speaking English "not at all," "not well" or "well") over the age of five in the United States, accounting for 9 percent of the total population. Nearly 52 percent (or 20.5 million) of the 39.7 million foreign-born persons age five and older were LEP. Spanish-speaking LEP individuals accounted for 66 percent (or 16.5 million) of the total LEP population. The next most common LEP languages were Mandarin and Cantonese (1.5 million, or 6 percent) and Vietnamese (836,000, or 3 percent).[10]

FACT:
Nearly 9 percent of the U.S. population has limited English proficiency.

What percentage of the adult foreign-born U.S. population is college educated?

In 2010 there were 33.6 million immigrants ages twenty-five and older in the United States. Of those, 27 percent had a bachelor's degree or higher (compared with more than 28 percent of 170.7 million native-born adults from the same age group), while nearly 32 percent lacked a high school diploma (compared to 11 percent of native-born adults).[11]

How has the emigration rate from Mexico changed over time?

Mexico's National Survey of Occupations and Employment (ENOE) asks Mexican households to declare any members of the household are who living abroad at the time of the interview. (It does not capture the emigration of entire families.) According to ENOE, the emigration rate from Mexico appears to have slowed recently, from 6.9 migrants per 1,000 residents of Mexico in the fall of 2008, to 5.4 per 1,000 in fall 2009, and 3.3 per 1,000 in fall 2010. In fall 2011 the emigration rate from Mexico increased slightly to 3.8 per 1,000 Mexico residents.

The immigration rate into Mexico (the number of people who move to Mexico from abroad, who are overwhelmingly return migrants) has entered a moderate decline, moving from 3.7 per 1,000 in fall 2008, to 2.1 per 1,000 three years later (fall 2011).

Has the United States ever encouraged Mexican laborers to immigrate?

The Immigration Act of 1917 restricted immigration from Asia, making it easier for Mexican laborers to find work in the United States, especially in agricultural, railroad, mining and construction sectors. This was considered the first *bracero* ("day laborer," "arm man" or "manual laborer") program.[12]

After World War I, Mexicans continued to be employed in the railroad and agriculture businesses. However, during the Great Depression migrants were the first to be laid off, and many Americans accused Mexican migrants of taking jobs from Americans.

The buildup to World War II generated new industrial jobs that attracted many Americans away from agricultural work. With insufficient American workers for the agricultural business, growers asked the U.S. Department of Agriculture (USDA) to "permit the importation of Mexican agricultural workers."[13] This second *bracero* program was initially administered by the USDA's War Food Administration's Office of Labor before being transferred to the Department of Labor in 1947.[14] It recruited Mexicans through newspaper, radio and word of mouth. Some 4.6 million Mexican workers were processed under this program.

FACT:
The immigration rate into Mexico has entered a moderate decline.

Does U.S. immigration policy tend to single out certain groups?

Unfortunately, U.S. immigration policy over time has directly singled out Chinese, Japanese and other Asian populations, as well as Eastern Europeans (especially Jews) and Mexicans. In many cases the policies were enacted with language stating that they were attempting to encourage positive aspects of the American experience or what was believed to be in the interest of American citizens, but in retrospect it is clear that many policies were highly prejudicial against certain populations.

"No Human Being Is Illegal!"

7. Immigration Reform

Almost everyone has an opinion about immigration. America has too many immigrants or too few. The U.S. immigration process is too strict or too lax. Immigrants are treated poorly or unfairly protected. It seems like something has to change, but there are many different ideas.

What is "immigration reform"?

Immigration reform means different things to different people, but there is almost universal agreement among people of both major U.S. political parties and many backgrounds that current immigration systems, processes, laws and procedures are badly broken. An independent report to Congress in 2012 begins, "There is a broad-based consensus that the US immigration system is broken."[1] According to former Florida governor Jeb Bush, "Our nation's immigration laws have been amended so many times that they have grown amazingly complex, incoherent, and sometimes self-contradictory."[2] President Barack Obama has said simply, "We've got to bring our legal immigration system into the 21st century."[3]

Some advocates contend that it is easier to immigrate illegally than legally because of the complexity of immigration laws and the relative ease of crossing the border, forging documents or simply overstaying a temporary visa.

What's wrong with the current U.S. immigration system?

There are a number of issues related to the current system. The complexity and changing nature of quotas, limits and even country preferences mean the average person has a difficult time negotiating the system even while they're in the United States. It is almost impossible to apply without the help of an attorney.

In addition, the complexity of the system has created backlogs of more than a decade in some categories as families wait for visas to be processed or for the quota limit in their category to clear. For many, the wait is such a hardship that they simply give up and enter the country illegally rather than spend a decade separated from their family.

There are some who question the priorities established by the categories, which favor reuniting family (including married adult children and siblings of immigrants) over individuals whose skills or assets could help grow the U.S. economy.

"There is a broad-based consensus that the U.S. immigration system is broken."

Ruth Ellen Wasem

Who is responsible for the mess?

U.S. laws are made by the legislative branch (Congress) but enforced by the executive branch (Departments of

State, Justice, Homeland Security, Treasury) and interpreted by the judicial branch (courts, from local to Supreme). Over the years, Congress has enacted laws that address current situations; these laws have formed more of a patchwork system than a comprehensive one.

Depending on the president and cabinet, the laws have been enforced in varying ways and have changed based on court rulings. Different courts interpret the law differently, and most immigration attorneys complain that immigration case rulings vary widely depending on the judge hearing the particular case.

> *"I do not believe the border is secure, and I still believe we have a long, long way to go."*
>
> Senator John Cornyn

Patrolling the U.S./Mexico border.

Haven't we already reformed immigration laws?

The last comprehensive reform of immigration occurred in 1990. The Immigration Act of 1990 revised the grounds for deportations and exclusions (which then included homosexuality), increased the number of legal immigrants who could enter the country annually from 500,000 to 700,000, revised categories for temporary (non-immigrant) visas and created the Diversity Visa Lottery Program (known as the "green card lottery"). The act also offered exceptions to the 1906 English language–testing requirement for all naturalized citizens.

What is immigration amnesty?

Immigration amnesty refers to the process of granting legal status to someone who either entered the United States illegally or has overstayed a temporary visa. In general, amnesty has been offered in the past or considered for the future only for people who meet certain conditions, such as having no illegal activity and having resided in the United States for a specified period of time.

Current proposals for immigration reform do not grant amnesty (although critics have described them as such). Instead they offer a way for undocumented workers to pay fines and meet certain criteria in order to enter the legal immigration process.

Has the United States ever granted amnesty to those living in the country illegally?

The Immigration Reform and Control Act of 1986 granted legal status to nearly 2 million undocumented immigrants who entered the United States before January 1, 1982, and had resided in the country continuously since then. As many as 1 million additional undocumented immigrants were granted amnesty under subsequent acts that expanded or clarified the 1986 act.

Gloria Estefan immigrated from Cuba.

The Nicaraguan Adjustment and Central American Relief Act of 1997 granted amnesty to Nicaraguans and Cubans, as well as undocumented immigrants from Guatemala, El Salvador and certain former Communist bloc countries (along with their spouses and unmarried children) who had lived in the United States illegally since 1995, as long as they applied for amnesty by April 1, 2000. That deadline has since been extended for certain cases.

The Haitian Refugee Immigration Fairness Act granted permanent resident status to any Haitians, along with their spouses and children, who had been in the United States since December 1995, as long as they applied before April 1, 2000.

What are the major issues being considered for immigration reform?

The main areas of immigration reform include increasing border security and immigration enforcement, modernizing legal immigration to promote both job creation and family unity, dealing with the undocumented population currently in the United States, and creating a process that is coordinated and transparent.

What are the specific proposals for immigration reform?

The most comprehensive proposal to date was introduced in the Senate in the spring of 2013. The Border Security, Economic Opportunity and Immigration Modernization Act—or S 744—was amended and eventually passed by the Senate that summer, then sent to the House of Representatives. The House failed to move the entire bill forward, although some representatives supported specific aspects of the comprehensive bill.

In summary, the main provisions of the Senate immigration reform bill call for:

FACT:
Most immigration reform proposals promote job creation.

1. **Improving border security**

    The most costly provision of the bill creates a fund of $46.3 billion to hire more border patrol agents, add 700 miles of fencing along the Mexican border, increase patrolling methods (including drones), add additional prosecutors and create a Southern Border Security Commission. The Commission would be responsible for recommending ways to keep the Mexican border secure.

    The fund also provides for more ways to prevent overstays, to implement E-Verify and to electronically track those exiting the United States.

    One of the most controversial aspects of this provision is the requirement that the effectiveness of these methods be measured and meet certain markers before any undocumented immigrants can gain legal status. Critics say this is unfair to those seeking legal status; proponents say it is the only way to be sure the border is secured effectively.

2. **Creating a "pathway to citizenship" or legal residency**

The aspect of the bill that has generated the most attention would allow those who are in the United States without documentation to follow a path that would provide legal residency and possibly citizenship. The bill creates a new status called "registered provisional immigrant" (RPI). Under the Senate bill, those who qualify for the RPI status could become U.S. citizens in as few as thirteen years. Some who oppose this provision have suggested that those who qualify should retain the RPI status, but supporters say that creates a permanent second-class resident.

Under this provision "DREAMers" would be offered an accelerated path to citizenship. Agricultural workers could qualify for a "blue card"—a new status for those who remain employed in agriculture.

3. **Reforming the legal immigration system**

The current immigration system primarily supports family unification, but critics say the United States has fallen behind other nations where immigration priority is given to those with technical skills and advanced degrees. The new program would set up a merit-based system, awarding points for education level, job skills, employment history, English proficiency and other qualifications. It would also eliminate the country-specific limits, which have backlogged highly skilled applicants from countries like China and India.

This aspect of the reform proposal also offers ways to clear up the backlog of the millions of applicants

"Yes, they broke the law. But it's not a felony. It's an act of love. It's an act of commitment to your family. . . . It shouldn't rile people up that people are actually coming to this country to provide for their families."

Jeb Bush

waiting in line to legally enter the United States and provides for their entry into the system before any of those who are currently in the United States illegally can move forward in the process.

But this provision eliminates certain categories such as siblings and married children (older than thirty) of U.S. citizens. It also creates a non-immigrant agricultural worker visa called a "W visa" that would allow for workers to come into the United States under specific conditions.

FACT:
Some immigration reform proposals set up a merit-based system for those seeking entry to the United States.

4. **Enforcing immigration laws and protecting immigrants**

   This aspect of the bill provides resources to enforce laws already in place and to implement and enforce the E-Verify system. It creates more severe penalties for immigrants involved in gangs and certain types of criminal activity, and makes individuals ineligible for RPI status if they have violated certain laws.

   It also provides greater protection for refugees and asylum seekers as well as victims of human trafficking and abuse in the workplace. It also provides, in some cases, for better representation of immigrants detained or facing deportation.

5. **Reforming non-immigrant visa programs**

   The bill offers more opportunities for visitors to the United States to invest or work, even if they don't intend to become permanent residents or citizens. This is especially important for multinational corporations who want to transfer workers among locations, as well as industries in which lower-skilled workers are needed (such as the hospitality industry).

   The bill also allows ways for students to stay in the United States and move from student visa status to more permanent status, and allows retirees to live in the United States if they can prove they have health coverage and sufficient financial means.

Would the reforms in this plan be costly?

The Congressional Budget Office (CBO) analyzed the plan and stated that the bill, if implemented into law, would have a net positive effect of nearly $1 trillion over the 2014–2033 period. While implementing some aspects of the plan is costly, the benefits would come from the increased size of the labor force by way of taxes, as well as the collection of back taxes and fines from the currently undocumented workers. The CBO states that the implementation of the plan would increase the U.S. gross domestic product (GDP) by 5.4 percent by 2033.

FACT:
The Immigration Act of 1990 was the last significant revision of legal permanent immigration.

How many of the current undocumented residents would qualify for the pathway to legal status?

Even if the proposed Senate bill were to pass the House, the requirements for moving into registered provisional immigrant status would eliminate many of the 11.7 million people currently residing in the United States illegally. The first hurdle is proving residency in the United States before December 31, 2011, then submitting to fingerprinting and a criminal background check. Any felonies or misdemeanors could automatically disqualify an individual, including using false documents or failing to register for the selective service. The next hurdle includes paying fines and back taxes. Then the

applicant must provide proof of employment or adequate resources to live above the poverty line. Applicants must also meet English proficiency requirements.

Meanwhile, anyone in RPI status is ineligible for public benefits, including Medicaid, food stamps or health coverage under the Affordable Care Act.

Those who qualify for RPI status must maintain it for ten years before applying for a legal permanent resident status. It would take another three years after that to apply for citizenship (if all other provisions are met).

How will immigrants manage all of these requirements?

Some critics of the plan say that the requirements would make it impossible for most undocumented residents to navigate the system without legal and other assistance.

A provision of the Senate bill includes the creation of three new organizations: the Office of Citizenship, to promote training and integration of new immigrants; the Task Force on New Americans, to coordinate the government response to immigration issues; and the U.S. Citizenship Foundation to provide assistance to individuals applying for RPI or LPR status.

How would immigration reform affect American workers and employers?

For most employers, the greatest impact would be the need to implement the E-Verify system. Multinational organizations would potentially have more freedom to move workers among locations, and tech companies and other employers would be able to recruit highly skilled and educated workers from other countries. Those in agricultural industries would have more opportunities to employ workers either temporarily or under new visa programs, and other industries, such as hospitality, would be able to recruit workers from overseas. Universities would have more opportunities to keep highly educated foreign students in the United States after they completed their degrees.

FACT:
Many countries attract more highly educated workers because of their immigration policies.

Why is there so much attention on the "pathway to citizenship"?

The "pathway to citizenship" describes one or more plans to create a process by which the more than 11 million current undocumented residents of the United States could move from illegal to legal immigration status with the possibility of eventually becoming citizens.

While some critics consider the process unfair because it allows those who have broken the law to remain in the United States, others say proposals for mass deportation would be impractical and harmful to the U.S. economy. Even the most generous proposals call on immigrants to pay fines and back taxes, prove employment and residency, and wait "at the back of the line" behind others who entered the country legally.

"Our land should be one of assimilation, not hiding in the shadows."

Senator
Rand Paul

The path to citizenship is also dependent on a timetable for federal enforcement of borders, employment verifications and better policing of those entering the country with visas. Another possible provision would require immigrants to show some proficiency in English before receiving a green card (there is no such requirement for current green card holders), so that they could assimilate more readily and have the opportunity to earn more money.

Some critics say such provisions will overwhelm most immigrants, who will be unable to pay the fines, fees and taxes, as well as hire an immigration attorney to negotiate the process. Others point out that making immigrants wait for all of the conditions to be met by the government puts them into an unfair and potentially long-term limbo status.

What parts of the government are involved in immigration issues?

The Departments of State, Treasury, Justice, Homeland Security, and Health & Human Services are all directly involved in immigration processing and enforcement. Other offices are also involved, such as the Department of Transportation, which oversees border crossings.

States primarily oversee areas such as education, so the responsibility for educating immigrant children falls to states. Also managed at the state level are drivers' licenses and healthcare benefits and costs.

What will happen to the "green card lottery"?

The Diversity Visa (DV) Lottery Program was authorized in 1990 and has made 50,000 lawful permanent resident ("green card") visas available each year to nationals of countries that the U.S. government considers to be underrepresented in U.S. immigration (those having fewer than 50,000 entries the previous year). The list of countries changes annually based on the previous year's immigration statistics, but countries like Mexico, China, the Philippines, India, the Dominican Republic and several others are usually excluded because of the high number of immigrants already coming from those countries. Anyone who is not from an excluded country can apply, whether they are currently within or outside the United States, although some restrictions apply.

The lottery has become so popular that as many as 8 million people apply for the 50,000 spots each year. In order to prioritize the immigration of more highly skilled workers, it is one of the programs that will likely be cut under immigration reform. Some critics claim this will hurt immigrants from countries in Africa, especially, who may lack the ability to qualify under a merit-based system.

FACT: *Unauthorized residents of the United States will have to pay fines and back taxes as part of immigration reform.*

Why have so many immigrants been deported in recent years?

According to U.S. Citizenship and Immigration Services, a record number of immigrants living in the United States illegally were deported in 2012. The majority of the 400,000 were deported because of illegal activities, but others had no charges against them except that they were residing in the country illegally. Critics say that many of those deported might have qualified to become legal residents under immigration reform.

What is the difference between the DREAM Act and DACA?

FACT:
The DREAM Act applies to individuals who are thirty years of age or younger.

The DREAM (Development, Relief and Education for Alien Minors) Act was first introduced in the U.S. Senate in 2001 and has been reintroduced in both the House and Senate several times.

The DREAM Act applies to individuals who are thirty or younger and who came to the United States before they turned sixteen, have lived in the United States continuously, have not been convicted of any crimes and are either currently enrolled in university or have recently graduated, or were honorably discharged from the military. Those who qualify are allowed to remain in the United States and receive work permits for at least two years.

The DREAM Act has not been passed by Congress and is expected to be part of the larger immigration reform legislation. In 2012, President Obama announced that young people who met the DREAM Act requirements would not be deported under a program called DACA. Almost every immigration proposal includes some provision to cover young people who qualify. Until a bill is passed into law, the federal government (which controls deportations) can protect these young people but cannot provide them with the pathway to citizenship most would prefer.

FACT:
DACA stands for Deferred Action for Childhood Arrivals.

What about those who already hold green cards? Will anything change for them as a result of immigration reform?

The nearly 15 million lawful permanent residents (LPRs) of the United States will not experience any changes as a result of immigration reform proposals. One proposal limits the number of family visas available to LPRs, shifting the greater percentage to naturalized citizens. Under the Affordable Care Act of 2010, lawful permanent residents are required to have health insurance and are restricted from receiving Medicaid until they have lived in the United States for five years.

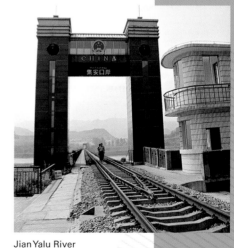

Jian Yalu River border crossing.

Why aren't green card holders deported if they commit a crime?

Although it is more difficult to deport lawful permanent residents than those who have not received a green card, there are still conditions under which a LPR will be deported. A person is subject to additional scrutiny during the first five years after being admitted to the United States, and can be deported if convicted of theft, burglary, assault or any crime that would call for jail time of one year or more. After the first five years of LPR status, removal is generally predicated on being convicted of two or more such crimes, having a drug-related offense or being convicted of an aggravated felony.

Why can't the United States change "birthright citizenship," as other countries have done?

Some believe that the United States will always have an immigration problem as long as the principle of *jus soli* (being born on U.S. soil) is in effect. As the wealthiest country in the world with this policy, the United States is attractive to many people from poor countries.

Some constitutional scholars believe *jus soli* is granted by the Fourteenth Amendment and that changing citizenship policy would require a constitutional amendment. Others contend that the amendment was specifically written to cover the rights of freed slaves, not immigrants; the application of the amendment to immigrant status has never been litigated. Without a ruling by the Supreme Court, the amendment remains open to interpretation.

Is legal immigration really that complicated?

U.S. immigration law is very complicated and confusing. Current law provides for an annual worldwide limit of 675,000 permanent immigrants, with certain exceptions for close family members and the available number of family preference visas for any given year.

After family relationships, the next level of priority for immigration is employment. Workers may enter the United States on either a temporary or a permanent basis. There are more than twenty types of temporary visas, some with numerical limits. Permanent

Family-Based Immigration System

Preference	U.S. Sponsor	Relationship	Numerical Limit
"Immediate Relatives"	U.S.-citizen adults	Spouses, unmarried minor children and parents	Unlimited
Total Family-Sponsored Visas Allocation			**480,000**
1	U.S. citizen	Unmarried adult children	23,400*
2A	LPR	Spouses and minor children	87,900
2B	LPR	Unmarried adult children	26,300
3	U.S. citizen	Married adult children	23,400**
4	U.S. citizen	Brothers and sisters	65,000***

* Plus any unused visas from the 4th preference
** Plus any unused visas from 1st and 2nd preferences
***Plus any unused visas from all other family-based preferences

employment-based immigration is presently capped at 140,000 visas per year, divided into five preferences. In addition to the category limits placed on the various immigration preferences, the Immigration and Nationality Act (INA) also places a limit on how many immigrants can come to the United States from any one country. A separate number is set annually for refugees and is usually between 60,000 and 80,000, and there are an unlimited number of spots for asylum seekers.

What is "self-deportation"?

Self-deportation refers to a voluntary return of un-documented immigrants to their home countries. The 2012 Republican Party platform called for "humane procedures to encourage illegal aliens to return home voluntarily."

What happens if no new legislation passes on immigration?

Until immigration reform is enacted, those living in the United States without documentation continue to live in limbo. While the executive branch sets policy about deportations, with each new administration the rules could change. Even without legislation it's likely that border security will be tightened up and employers will be more likely to implement E-Verify, making jobs more difficult to secure without documentation.

Families will continue to be separated and legal immigration will continue to be backlogged. Businesses will struggle to find highly skilled workers and some industries will have a hard time finding enough workers to meet growing demands. Long term, the negative implications of failing to pass immigration reform are great for individuals, communities and businesses.

Permanent Employment-Based Preference System

Preference Category	Eligibility	Yearly Numerical Limit
Total Employment-Based Immigrants		140,000 for principals and their dependents
1	"Persons of extraordinary ability" in the arts, science, education, business or athletics; professors and researchers; some multinational executives.	40,000*
2	Members of the professions holding advanced degrees, or persons of exceptional abilities in the arts, science or business.	40,000**
3	Skilled shortage workers with at least two years of training or experience, professionals with college degrees, or "other" workers for unskilled labor that is not temporary or seasonal.	40,000*** "Other" unskilled laborers restricted to 5,000
4	Certain "special immigrants," including religious workers, employees of U.S. foreign service posts, former U.S. government employees and other classes of aliens.	10,000
5	Persons who will invest $500,000 to $1 million in a job-creating enterprise that employs at least ten full-time U.S. workers.	10,000

*Plus any unused visas from the 4th and 5th preferences
**Plus any unused visas from the 1st preference
***Plus any unused visas the 1st and 2nd preferences

A Coast Guard boat patrols the waters around New York City with the Statue of Liberty in the background.

Conclusion

It's tempting to think that the current debate about immigration is simply one more aspect of America's polarized political landscape. But when you look at the history of the country, it becomes clear that immigration issues have divided Americans from our very earliest days. Almost from the beginning we asked, "Who belongs here and who doesn't?" The answer to that question has changed over the years, but the fundamental issue remains: Is America truly a melting pot, a place where anyone from anywhere in the world can make a home? Or is it a country only open to those who fit a certain norm or are able to contribute to society in measurable ways?

Other nations also ask these questions. Many have created laws to sort out who may stay and who must go, and have even changed their basic rules of immigration. Some countries have found ways to entice individuals with special skills, talents and capital. Other countries have found ways to bring in workers when needed without granting rights and privileges reserved for their citizens. As wars expand and disasters strike, some countries throw open their doors to welcome those in need, while others are more cautious about who they let in and for how long.

With the ease of travel and availability of information, it's natural that individuals search for a new home if their own country lacks opportunity. Some have a relatively easy transition to a new land. Others wander for years or end up stuck in a refugee camp or worse. The movement of people creates opportunity for the unscrupulous and criminals to prey on those who have no protection and no permanent home.

Migration of peoples continues at an accelerated rate, and countries increasingly struggle to adjust. In the United States, the debate rages on, sometimes politically but also personally. Is it a matter of compassion or fairness? Are we asking what is good for the majority or the minority? Prayers and voices are raised while individuals struggle to plan for their present and future.

And while we debate what act of legislation can solve this problem, on some level we know that we are just reacting to the latest issue. Today's solution will be tomorrow's challenge. Those people we welcome now may be the ones who turn against the immigrants of the future, seeing them as different, less desirable, more like "them" and less like "us." It has happened throughout our history, and there is little reason to believe it won't happen again.

So we continue to discuss what is one of the most fundamental issues of democracy. Who we are as a nation is determined not only by the will of our current citizens but also by the rules we set for those knocking at our door. Just as America has been shaped by immigrants of the past, it will be influenced in the future by who we exclude, who we allow in and who we truly welcome.

My hope is that this book will help us all make those decisions with more facts than emotions, and more awareness than fear. And I pray that it will serve as a guide for more debates and fewer arguments about the complex subject of immigration.

Notes

Introduction

[1]From Emma Lazarus, "The New Colossus," inscribed on the Statue of Liberty.

Chapter One: Defining Terms

[1]This number does not include more than 5 million Palestinian refugees who are counted separately under a different agency. UNHCR, "The State of the World's Refugees," accessed September 10, 2013, www.unhcr.org/4fc5ceca9.html.

[2]International Convention on the Protection of the Rights of All Migrant Workers and Members of Their Families, United Nations, December 18, 1990.

[3]Ruth Ellen Wasem, "US Immigration Policy: Chart Book of Key Trends," Congressional Research Service, March 7, 2013, p. 7.

Chapter Two: The Big Picture

[1]Revital Hovel, "Supreme Court Asked to Rethink Ruling That Nationality May Not Be Changed from 'Jewish' to 'Israeli,'" *Haaretz,* October 20, 2013.

[2]Dahr Jamail, "Jordan to Host 'World's Largest Refugee Camp,'" Al Jazeera, May 16, 2013, accessed December 23, 2013, www.aljazeera.com/humanrights/2013/05/20135136445430108.html.

[3]Convention Relating to the Status of Refugees, United Nations, July 28, 1951, Article 33(1).

[4]Julie Scheeres, "ID Cards Are de Rigeur Worldwide," *Wired,* September 25, 2001, accessed May 15, 2013, www.wired.com/politics/law/news/2001/09/47073.

[5]Tarun Wadhwa, "We Don't Need a National ID Card," *Forbes,* February 6, 2013, accessed May 15, 2013, www.forbes.com/sites/tarunwadhwa/2013/02/06/the-washington-post-got-it-wrong-we-dont-need-a-national-id-card/.

[6]"U.N.: 2.4 Million Human Trafficking Victims," accessed August 19, 2013, http://usatoday30.usatoday.com/news/world/story/2012-04-03/human-trafficking-sex-UN/53982026/1.

Chapter Three: A Nation of Immigrants

[1]Adam Ozimek, "Is the US the Most Immigrant Friendly Nation in the World?" *Forbes,* November 18, 2012, accessed May 3, 2012, www.forbes.com/sites

/modeledbehavior/2012/11/18/is-the-u-s-the-most-immigrant-friendly-country-in-the-world/.

[2]Jeffrey S. Passel, D'vera Cohn and Ana Gonzalez-Barrera, "Population Decline of Unauthorized Immigrants Stalls, May Have Reversed," September 23, 2013, accessed October 24, 2013, www.pewhispanic.org/2013/09/23/population-decline-of-unauthorized-immigrants-stalls-may-have-reversed.

[3]Ruth Ellen Wasem, "Nonimmigrant Overstays: Brief Synthesis of the Issue," Congressional Research Service, January 15, 2010, p. 4, accessed May 30, 2013, www.crs.gov.

[4]Alison Sisken, "The Visa Waiver Program," Congressional Research Service, January 15, 2013, p. 9.

[5]"US Naturalizations: 2012," Homeland Security, Office of Immigration Statistics, March 2013, accessed May 10, 2013, www.dhs.gov/immigration-statistics.

[6]U.S. Citizenship and Immigration Services, "Naturalization Fact Sheet," October 24, 2012, accessed May 23, 2013, www.uscis.gov.

[7]James Lee, "U.S. Naturalizations: 2012," Annual Flow Report, Department of Homeland Security, March 2013, accessed August 19, 2013, www.dhs.gov/sites/default/files/publications/ois_natz_fr_2012.pdf.

[8]"US Immigration Laws and the Selective Service," Lawyers.com, accessed December 23, 2013, http://immigration.lawyers.com/immigration/us-immigration-laws-and-the-selective-service.html.

[9]Jack Maskell, "Qualifications for President and the 'Natural Born' Citizenship Eligibility Requirement," Congressional Research Service, November 14, 2011, p. 25.

Chapter Four: Major Issues Affecting U.S. Immigration

[1]Jeffrey S. Passel, D'vera Cohn and Ana Gonzalez-Barrera, "Population Decline of Unauthorized Immigrants Stalls, May Have Reversed," September 23, 2013, accessed December 23, 2013, www.pewhispanic.org/2013/09/23/population-decline-of-unauthorized-immigrants-stalls-may-have-reversed.

[2]American Immigration Council, "Immigrants and Crime: Are They Connected?" October 25, 2008, accessed December 23, 2013, www.immigrationpolicy.org/just-facts/immigrants-and-crime-are-they-connected-century-research-finds-crime-rates-immigrants-are.

[3]American Immigration Council, "From Anecdotes to Evidence: Setting the Record Straight on Immigrants and Crime," September 10, 2008, accessed December 23, 2013, www.immigrationpolicy.org/just-facts/anecdotes-evidence-setting-record-straight-immigrants-and-crime.

[4]See Jana Kasperkevic, "Deporting All of America's Illegal Immigrants Would Cost a Whopping $285 Billion," Business Insider, accessed December 23, 2013,

www.businessinsider.com/deporting-all-of-americas-illegal-immigrants-would-cost-a-whopping-285-billion-2012-1.

[5]Jim Barnett, "U.S. Deportations Reach Historic Levels," CNN, October 18, 2011, accessed December 23, 2013, www.cnn.com/2011/10/18/us/immigrant-deportations/.

[6]"The Shattered Families Report," Race Forward, November 2, 2011, www.race forward.org/research/reports/shattered-families.

[7]Brad Plumer, "Who's Crossing the Mexico Border?" *Wonkblog, Washington Post,* June 2, 2013, accessed December 23, 2013, www.washingtonpost.com/blogs/wonkblog/wp/2013/06/02/whos-crossing-the-mexico-border-a-new-survey-tries-to-find-out.

[8]Edwin Mora, "Canadian Border Bigger Terror Threat Than Mexican Border, Says Border Patrol Chief," CNSNews.com, May 18, 2011, accessed December 23, 2013, http://cnsnews.com/news/article/canadian-border-bigger-terror-threat-mexican-border-says-border-patrol-chief.

[9]Ashley Fantz, "The Mexico Drug War: Bodies for Billions," CNN.com, January 20, 2012, accessed December 23, 2013, www.cnn.com/2012/01/15/world/mexico-drug-war-essay.

[10]Suzy Khimm, "How Long Is the Immigration 'Line'? As Long as 24 Years," *Wonkblog, Washington Post,* January 31, 2013, accessed December 23, 2013, www.washingtonpost.com/blogs/wonkblog/wp/2013/01/31/how-long-is-the-immigration-line-as-long-as-24-years/.

[11]Annual Report of Immigrant Visa Applicants in the Family-Sponsored and Employment-Based Preferences Registered at the National Visa Center as of November 1, 2013, accessed December 23, 2013, www.travel.state.gov/content/dam/visas/Statistics/Immigrant-Statistics/WaitingListItem.pdf.

[12]Anna Schecter, "Born in the USA—Birth Tourists Get Instant U.S. Citizenship for Their Newborns," *Rock Center with Brian Williams,* May 7, 2013, accessed December 23, 2013, http://rockcenter.nbcnews.com/_news/2013/03/07/17225891-born-in-the-usa-birth-tourists-get-instant-us-citizenship-for-their-newborns?lite.

[13]The Evangelical Immigration Table, "Evangelical Statement of Principles for Immigration Reform," accessed December 23, 2013, www.evangelicalimmigration table.com/#principles.

Chapter Five: Economics of Immigration

[1]"Immigration and the Economy," White House, accessed March 5, 2014, www.whitehouse.gov/issues/immigration/economy.

[2]Ibid.

[3]Robert Lenzner, "40% of the Largest U.S. Companies Founded by Immigrants

or Their Children," *Forbes*, www.forbes.com/sites/robertlenzner/2013/04/25/40-largest-u-s-companies-founded-by-immigrants-or-their-children.

[4]Matt Cover, "Illegal Immigrants Account for $10.7 Billion of Nation's Health Care Costs, Data Show," CNSNews.com, July 29, 2009, http://cnsnews.com/news/article/illegal-immigrants-account-107-billion-nation-s-health-care-costs-data-show.

[5]Lance T. Izumi, "Educating Illegal Immigrants Is Costly," *Atlanta Journal-Constitution*, August 17, 2010, www.ajc.com/news/news/opinion/educating-illegal-immigrants-is-costly/nQjSw.

[6]Nicole Goodkind, "Immigration Reform Could Cost Social Security Billions," March 14, 2013, http://finance.yahoo.com/blogs/daily-ticker/social-security-risk-impact-immigration-reform-124712696.html.

[7]"Additional ITIN Information," accessed August 30, 2013, at www.irs.gov/Individuals/Additional-ITIN-Information.

[8]World Bank, "Remittances," accessed August 30, 2013, http://go.worldbank.org/JIMCZZTRK0.

[9]"Remittances: Over the Sea and Far Away," *The Economist*, May 19, 2012, www.economist.com/node/21554740.

[10]Western Union, "Western Union Highlights Strategic Initiatives at 2013 Annual Stockholders' Meeting," press release, May 30, 2013, http://ir.westernunion.com/News/Press-Releases/Press-Release-Details/2013/Western-Union-Highlights-Strategic-Initiatives-at-2013-Annual-Stockholders-Meeting/default.aspx.

Chapter Six: Who Are the Immigrants?

[1]"Salma Hayek: I Was an Illegal Immigrant," *Huffington Post*, December 9, 2010, accessed August 30, 2013, www.huffingtonpost.com/2010/12/09/salma-hayek-i-was-an-illegal-immigrant_n_794586.html.

[2]Julia Preston, "Risks Seen for Children of Illegal Immigrants," *New York Times*, September 20, 2011, accessed December 23, 2013, www.nytimes.com/2011/09/21/us/illegal-immigrant-parents-pass-a-burden-study-says.html?_r=0.

[3]Suzy Khimm, "How Long Is the Immigration 'Line'? As Long as 24 Years," *Wonkblog, Washington Post*, January 31, 2013, accessed August 30, 2013, www.washingtonpost.com/blogs/wonkblog/wp/2013/01/31/how-long-is-the-immigration-line-as-long-as-24-years/.

[4]Miranda Leitsinger, "Waiting Half a Life for a Green Card: Families Languish in Immigration Line," NBC News, April 12, 2013, accessed August 30, 2013, http://usnews.nbcnews.com/_news/2013/04/12/17709883-waiting-half-a-life-for-a-green-card-families-languish-in-immigration-line?lite. The wait time is longer for LPRs sponsoring children than it is for citizens.

[5]Department of Homeland Security, *Annual Flow Report,* May 2011, accessed December 23, 2013, www.dhs.gov/xlibrary/assets/statistics/publications/ois_rfa_ fr_2010.pdf.

[6]Leslie Berestein Rojas, "'Temporary Protected' Status Immigrants Hope to Be Included in Immigration Reform," Southern California Public Radio, April 8, 2013, accessed December 23, 2013, www.scpr.org/blogs/multiamerican/2013 /04/08/13207/permanent-temporary-immigrants-hope-to-be-included/.

[7]Jeffrey S. Passel and D'Vera Cohn, "Unauthorized Immigrant Population: National and State Trends, 2010," *Pew Research Hispanic Trends Project,* February 1, 2011, accessed August 30, 2013, www.pewhispanic.org/2011/02/01 /unauthorized-immigrant-population-brnational-and-state-trends-2010.

[8]Paul Taylor, Mark Hugo Lopez, Jeffrey S. Passel and Seth Motel, "Unauthorized Immigrants: Length of Residency, Patterns of Parenthood," *Pew Research Hispanic Trends Report,* December, 1, 2011, accessed August 30, 2013, www.pewhispanic .org/2011/12/01/unauthorized-immigrants-length-of-residency-patterns-of-parenthood.

[9]Jeffrey S. Passel and D'Vera Cohn, "A Portrait of Unauthorized Immigrants in the United States," *Pew Research Hispanic Trends Project,* April 14, 2009, accessed August 30, 2013, www.pewhispanic.org/2009/04/14/a-portrait-of-unauthorized-immigrants-in-the-united-states.

[10]Migration Policy Institute, "LEP Data Brief," December 2011, accessed September 3, 2013, www.migrationinformation.org/integration/LEPdatabrief.pdf.

[11]Migration Policy Institute, "2011 American Community Survey and Census Data on the Foreign Born by State," accessed September 3, 2013, www.migration information.org/datahub/acscensus.cfm.

[12]Barbara Driscoll, *The Tracks North* (Austin: University of Texas Press, 1999).

[13]Ibid., pp. 52-53.

[14]Erasmo Gamboa, *Mexican Labor and World War II* (Austin: University of Texas Press, 1990), pp. 41, 121.

Chapter Seven: Immigration Reform

[1]Ruth Ellen Wasem, "Overview of Immigration Issues in the 112th Congress," Congressional Research Service, January 12, 2012, p. 1.

[2]Jeb Bush and Clint Bolick, *Immigration Wars* (New York: Simon & Schuster, 2013), p. 14.

[3]"Streamlining Legal Immigration," White House, accessed March 5, 2014, www.whitehouse.gov/issues/immigration/streamlining-immigration.

Credits

Diagrams and photographs in this book are provided by the author, with the following exceptions:

p. 8: Refugees from the Democratic Republic of Congo. Photo by Kevin Cook, World Vision.

p. 10: Syrian children. Photo by Kevin Cook, World Vision.

p. 11: Albert Einstein. Photo by Library of Congress.

p. 14: Refugees arrive in Seattle. Photo by Amanda Winger.

p. 16: A woman resettled by World Relief. Photo by Sean Sheridan.

p. 21: A migrant worker from Africa. Photo by Sharon Ben-Arie.

p. 22: Former Secretary of State Madeleine Albright. Photo by NASA.

p. 26: Syrian refugees living in a U.N. camp. Photo by Kevin Cook, World Vision.

p. 32: After the 2010 earthquake. Photo by Kevin Cook, World Vision.

p. 46: An immigration reform rally. Photo by Ryan Roderick Beiler.

p. 50: Recent immigrants study for the citizenship test. Photo by Sean Sheridan, World Vision.

p. 85: Photo by Steve Jeter, Sojourners.

p. 77: Young people rally for the DREAM Act. Photo by Todd Dwyer.

p. 86: A union marches for immigration reform. Photo by Steve Rhodes.

p. 89: Google cofounder Sergey Brin. Photo by Steve Jurvetson.

p. 92: Money remittance sign. Photo by FutureAtlas.com.

p. 102: Photo by Thomas Hawk.

p. 122: Photo by Ryan Roderick Beiler.

About the Author

Dale Hanson Bourke is president of PDI, a marketing and communications strategy firm. The author of ten books and numerous magazine articles, she often speaks and writes on international development and women's issues. Previously president of the CIDRZ Foundation and SVP at World Relief, Bourke has also served as publisher of Religion News Service and editor of *Today's Christian Woman*, and was a nationally syndicated columnist.

A graduate of Wheaton College, Dale holds an MBA from the University of Maryland and has served on the boards of World Vision US, World Vision International, International Justice Mission, Sojourners, ECFA and Opportunity International. She currently serves on the board of MAP International and the Center for Interfaith Action on Global Poverty (CIFA).

www.DaleHansonBourke.com
Twitter: @DaleHBourke
Facebook: facebook.com/SkepticsGuides

The Skeptic's Guide™ Series

Do you wish you understood some of the most complicated issues of our times? Would you like help navigating these sometimes divisive subjects? Then the Skeptic's Guide™ series is for you. Each book answers the most often asked questions, illustrating concepts with photos and charts, and even showing different points of view.

The Israeli-Palestinian Conflict sheds light on the places, terms, history and current issues shaping this important region, providing a framework for Christians to use in understanding why the conflict occurred, why it continues—and what remains to be done.

Responding to HIV/AIDS explains this complex question in lay terms, discussing science, politics and the response of everyone from governments to churches. This is the most up-to-date version of the guide that has become required reading for anyone dealing with HIV and AIDS.

The Israeli-Palestinian Conflict
(available now)

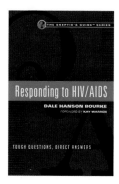

Responding to HIV/AIDS
(available now)

www.ivpress.com/skepticsguides